Also by Blanche Knott
Published by St. Martin's Press

Blanche Knott's

Truly Tasteless Jokes VIII

ST. MARTIN'S PRESS/NEW YORK

TRULY TASTELESS JOKES VIII

Copyright © 1988 by Blanche Knott

Library of Congress Catalog Card Number: 87-50347

ISBN: 0-312-91058-4   Can. ISBN: 0-312-91059-2

Printed in the United States of America

First St. Martin's Press mass market edition/July 1988

10 9 8 7 6 5 4 3 2 1

for WRE & EJ

POLISH

What does a Polish bride get on her wedding night that's long and hard?

A new last name.

•

Six Polish men rented a house together, and it didn't take long for them to detect that the house was infested with rats. So one night, armed with baseball bats and any other weapons they could get their hands on, they went down to the basement to do battle with their unwelcome guests.

Three weeks later, having failed to reach any of his tenants by telephone, the landlord used his key to enter the house. Finding only one badly beaten man, he cried, "Good God, what happened? And where are the other five?"

"Two were killed in action," croaked the battered Pole, "and the other three ran off with war brides."

•

How many Poles does it take to unstop a toilet?
  Three. Two to hold his legs and one to dive and suck.

•

A Pole's house is furiously burning down, surrounded by fire trucks and helpless firemen, and all the Pole can do is stand by and laugh and laugh. So his neighbor comes over and says, "Jerzy, your house is being burned down to the foundations and you're *laughing?*"

  "Why not?" says Jerzy with a chuckle. "I got enough wood in the attic to build another one."

•

Then there is Zabriskie, who approaches his friend Zalewski with a big bag and says, "Zalewski, if you can guess how many chickens I have in this bag, I'll give you both of them."

  "Three," pronounces Zalewski.

  Zabriskie pouts. "No fair, you peeked."

•

Why don't Poles like dancing cheek to cheek?
  Their asses get sore.

•

Why did the Pole drive around the block fifty-seven times?
  His turn signal was stuck.

•

Hear about the Pole who tried to hijack a submarine?
  He demanded $250,000 and a parachute.

•

How about the one who got his cock stuck in his car's battery?

He was told he had to jump it in order to get the car started.

•

Or the Pole who thought he was bisexual?

His girlfriend wouldn't put out, so he had to pay for it.

•

Seen the Polish dog-carrier?

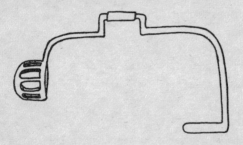

•

Two Poles were watching a football game on TV when a commercial for Tucks Hemorrhoidal Medicated Pads came on, showing a lit match being extinguished in a moist pad. "Tucks Medicated Pads relieve the burning and itching of hemorrhoidal tissue," said the soothing voice-over.

"I've got to buy myself some of those," said the first Pole, confiding that his hemorrhoids had really been bothering him.

"Well, what do you expect," cried his buddy, "when you keep sticking lit matches up your ass!"

•

3

What's the first thing Poles do after a wedding?
   Flush the punch bowl.

•

How can it be proved that Adam was Polish?
   Who else would stand by a naked woman and just eat an apple?

•

A Pole went to the corner drugstore and was shocked to find that a single pencil cost thirty cents. Venting his indignation on the cashier, he said loudly, "Listen, before you rip me off, are you sure this pencil works?"

•

How do you brainwash a Polish woman?
   Step on her douche bag.

•

One day a Polish woman who happened to know a bit of Spanish was walking down the street and passed a Cuban pervert. Winking lewdly at her, he said, "Hola, mam!"
   With a big smile, the woman turned around and said, "Hi, son!"

•

Did you hear about the Pole who thought Johnny Cash was a pay toilet?

•

A young Pole got off the plane on his first visit to the U.S. and was walking through JFK International Airport when he was approached by a religious fanatic in a white gown. The man handed the visitor a flower, rolled his eyes a bit, and asked, "Have you found Jesus?"

"Found Him?" asked the bewildered Pole. "How the hell could I do that? He's been dead for two thousand years."

•

Did you hear about the Pole who broke his leg playing golf?
He fell off the ball wash.

•

How about the Polish kid whose teacher told him to write a one hundred word essay on what he did during summer vacation?
He wrote "Not much" fifty times.

•

What happens when you double-cross the Polish Mafia?
They cast your feet in blocks of cement and throw you into a wading pool.

•

One morning I saw my friend Kowalski's father up early taking out the garbage. "Say, what're you doing?" I asked.
He answered, "Moving."

•

Hear about the Pole who didn't dare serve tea to his visitors?
He didn't have a T-shirt!

•

5

Little old Mrs. Brezinski was taking her constitutional around the block when a flasher jumped out from behind a tree and opened his coat wide.

"Oh, dear," she sighed, after surveying what the man had to offer, "now I suppose you're going to want me to show you mine. . . ."

•

Why did the Pole take a leak in the middle of the cafeteria?
  He saw a sign that read WET FLOOR.

•

Know why the Polish plane crashed?
  It ran out of coal.

•

Why aren't there any golf courses in Poland?
  Because most Poles don't know their asses from a hole in the ground.

•

What am I? [Stick your fingers in your ears and hop up and down as hard as you can.]
  A Polish mine detector.

•

Two little Polish girls were walking down the block to school and one said to the other, "Hey, know what I found on the patio the other day? A contraceptive."
  "Oh yeah?" said her friend. "What's a patio?"

•

Did you hear about the Pole who went to the bar and ordered seven White Russians?

He was trying to get them to defect.

•

How do they list the deaths in the *Warsaw Times?*

Under "Civic Improvements."

•

When Mr. Petrowski realized he was having trouble reading road signs, he knew it was time to visit the eye doctor and get his first pair of glasses. Seating him in front of the eye chart, the ophthalmologist instructed his patient to cover one eye with his hand. But despite the doctor's repeated instructions, Mr. Petrowski seemed incapable of anything other than a saluting motion.

Finally the ophthalmologist lost all patience. Fashioning a mask out of a brown paper bag and cutting out a hole for one eye, he put it over the man's head. "How does that feel, Mr. Petrowski?" he asked.

After a little pause Petrowski answered, "The fit is fine, Doctor, but I confess I was hoping for something a little more stylish, maybe with a tortoiseshell frame?"

•

If Tarzan and Jane were Polish, what would Cheetah be?

The smartest of the three.

•

What were Jesus' last instructions to the Polish people?

"Play dumb till I get back."

•

7

"No, Jerzy," said Stella when her boyfriend asked her to go jogging. "I'm not feeling too well."

"Whaddaya mean, not feeling well?"

"You know," she explained, blushing a bit, "it's that time of the month."

"Whaddaya mean, that time of the month?"

"You know," she went on, "I have my period."

"Whaddaya mean, period?"

"You know, Jerzy," Stella blurted in exasperation. "I'm bleeding down there!" And she lifted her skirt to show him.

"No wonder," he screamed in horror. "Someone's cut your cock off!"

•

Why did the Pole name his dog Herpes?

Because it wouldn't heel.

•

The basketball coach stormed into the university president's office and demanded a raise right then and there.

"Jesus Christ, man," protested President Kubritski, "you already make more than the entire English department."

"Yeah, maybe so, but you don't know what I have to put up with," the coach blustered. "Watch this." He went out into the hall and grabbed a jock who was jogging down the hallway. "Run over to my office and see if I'm there," he ordered.

Twenty minutes later the jock returned, sweaty and out of breath. "You're not there, sir," he reported.

"Oh, I see what you mean," conceded President Kubritski, scratching his head. "*I* would have phoned."

•

What's the most useless thing on a Polish woman?

A Polish man.

•

What does a Pole think 7–11 is?
  An emergency number.

•

So why don't they use the 911 system in Poland?
  The Poles can't find the eleven on their telephone dials.

•

Two young Polish hitchhikers were picked up by a farmer, who motioned to them to sit in the back of his pickup truck. The boys jumped in and were enjoying the breeze when suddenly a front tire blew, causing the truck to veer off the road and into a pond.

The farmer got out of the cab and swam to shore, where he turned and watched for the two riders to come to the surface. But as the minutes ticked by he began to lose hope, figuring that they must have drowned. Just as he was turning away, the two boys emerged, sputtering and choking, and made their way to the shore.

"What took you guys so long?" asked the farmer, thumping them on the back. "I figured you were goners."

Still gasping for breath, the boys explained, "Couldn't get the tailgate down."

JEWISH

An extremely pale, slight man wearing dark glasses stood out from the usual crowd by a Miami Beach pool. Mrs. Kravitz took an immediate interest in the newcomer. Settling herself next to his deck chair, she introduced herself and asked, "Why so pale?"

"Leave me alone, lady," grunted the man. "I just got outta jail."

"Oh, I see," said Mrs. Kravitz, pursing her lips. "How long were you in for?"

"Five years."

"That's terrible," she clucked. "For what?"

"Embezzlement."

"Ooh." Mrs. Kravitz nodded knowledgeably.

"And then five years for armed robbery," said the man in a sudden burst of talkativeness, "and then another lousy ten."

"And what was that for?"

"I killed my wife."

A big smile coming over her face, Mrs. Kravitz sat bolt

11

upright. "Myrna," she shouted to her friend across the pool, "he's *single!*"

•

Did you hear about the Jewish porn movie?
  It's called *Debbie Does Bubkis*.

•

What do you call an uncircumcised Jewish baby?
  A girl.

•

The matchmaker had been trying for years to find someone for young Seymour, but nobody came up to Mrs. Schwartz's standards. One day she showed up for her visit in an unusually good mood. "Have I got the girl for your Seymour," she announced, leaning over conspiratorially. "Nothing less than a princess, Princess Margaret Rose!" Ignoring the fact that Mrs. Schwartz had turned pale, the matchmaker went on. "She's a *lovely* girl. She has her own palace right on the Côte d'Azur, plus a chalet for the winter season in Gstaad, and of course there's the penthouse in Manhattan if you should get lonely for your son—"

"But wait, she's a shiksa," interrupted Mrs. Schwartz. "That's totally unacceptable."

"Let me tell you a little about the palace. Sixty-five rooms, not counting the servants' quarters or stables, and maybe you'd like to ice-skate or take a dip in a nice indoor Olympic-sized pool? Rembrandts and Caravaggios everywhere, and on the grounds—"

"Listen to me," broke in Mrs. Schwartz. "A Gentile girl, I don't care who she is, is absolutely out of the question."

"And maybe your Seymour likes a nice car?" The matchmaker went on, unperturbed. "In the garage is a Rolls-Royce, a Ferrari, a Maserati, and of course the two Mer-

12

cedes used for errands around town. And there's a couple of chauffeurs in case Seymour should get tired of driving . . ."

The ongoing inventory of Princess Margaret Rose's attractions, physical and material, failed to remove the frown from Mrs. Schwartz's face. Finally the matchmaker said, "Listen, let's give the boy a chance to hear all this for himself."

Reluctantly Mrs. Schwartz agreed. To Seymour, sitting on the couch next to his mother, the matchmaker once again patiently catalogued the splendor of all that Princess Margaret Rose, shiksa or not, had to offer.

"Ma, I gotta say it doesn't sound so bad," admitted Seymour.

It took another good hour or so but finally the matchmaker and Seymour persuaded Mrs. Schwartz to go along with the arrangement, and with much handshaking and back patting, the matchmaker was shown to the door.

"Well," she said as it closed behind her, "at least *half* my job is done."

•

What's the difference between an Israelite and an Israeli?
   About thirty calories.

•

Why are synagogues round?
   So there are no corners to hide in when the collection plate is passed.

•

What do you call a thousand JAPs on a sale day at Bloomingdale's?
   Yidlock.

•

13

What does a Southern Jew say?
  "*Chai,* y'all!"

•

Why does a Jewish divorce cost so much?
  It's worth it.

•

What's "perfect sex" to a JAP?
  Simultaneous headaches.

•

What's so special about the elevator at Bloomingdale's?
  It's about the only thing a JAP will go down on.

•

A devout Jew, Mrs. Feinstein offered up her prayers each week in temple. One week she prayed especially fervently. "Lord, I have always been a good Jew, and I've had a good life. I only have one complaint: I'm poor. Please, Lord, let me win the lottery."

The next week, Mrs. Feinstein was a little more strident. "Lord," she prayed, "have I ever missed a High Holy Day? Not fasted on Yom Kippur? Why must I go to my grave a pauper? One lottery win is all I'm asking You for."

The third week Mrs. Feinstein made no bones about her displeasure. "A faithful Jew such as myself, Lord, always observant, always dutiful, asks for one little favor, and what do I get. . . ?"

A glowing, white-bearded figure stepped down from the heavens into the temple. "Now, Mrs. Feinstein," boomed God, "don't you think you could at least meet me halfway, and buy a ticket?"

BLACK

What do you call a white man who dies and gets wings?
  An angel.
How about a black man who does the same?
  A bat.

•

Toby and Rastus were fighting over Annie, so she decided to settle matters once and for all. "You two race across the river," she pronounced, "and whoever wins gets to be my man."

The two men agreed to the contest, walked across the bridge to the far bank, and jumped in. As they were swimming, Annie decided she was partial to Rastus, so when he next looked up she hiked up her skirt a bit.

Rastus slowed down.

The next time he looked up she pulled her skirt up to her waist (she had no drawers on), and Rastus stopped dead in the middle of the river. "Rastus, what's the matter?" she cried.

"Goddamn, woman, put that dress down!" howled Rastus. "My rudder is stuck in the mud."

•

What was the first government-subsidized housing program?
  Uncle Tom's cabin.

•

What do you call a white man surrounded by three blacks?
  Victim.

•

What do you call a white man surrounded by five blacks?
  Coach.

•

What do you call a white man surrounded by ten blacks?
  Quarterback.

•

And what do you call a white man surrounded by three hundred blacks?
  Warden.

•

Did you hear about the nervous black bank robber?
  He went up to the teller and said, "All right, you mothersticker, this is a fuckup!"

•

A little black kid decided to enter a cock contest sponsored by a local bar. When he walked in the door that night carry-

16

ing a huge trophy, his mother asked how he had won it.

"I entered this contest to see who had the biggest cock, Ma," explained the kid. "The first white guy pulled out a cock that measured ten inches. The second white guy pulled one out that measured fifteen inches. Then it was my—"

The boy's mother interrupted him with a scream of alarm. "My God, Joey, you didn't pull that whole thing out, now did you?"

"Hell no, Ma," said Joey bashfully, "just enough to win."

•

What do you call a Kenyan waitress in a Playboy Club?
  A jungle bunny.

•

Hear about the new, all-black western?
  It's going to be called *Ride, Motherfucker, Ride*.

•

A black guy had been waiting for the bus for at least half an hour when he was overcome by the need to take a shit. He didn't want to use the rest room of the gas station across the way for fear of missing the bus, so he tried to hold on. But soon it became a matter of go or bust. In desperation he pulled down his pants and let go, right there on the sidewalk.

Not too much later, the bus pulled up and the door opened.

"How much is the fare into the city?" asked the black.

"$2.25," replied the bus driver, "and $1.50 for your little brother."

•

On the first day of school the teacher asked the little boy his name. "Osborne Green," said the little boy.

"You're off to the principal's office if you don't tell me your real name," snarled the teacher.

So he was dragged into the principal's office, where he protested, "My name is Osborne Green."

"You tell the truth or you'll have to leave school," threatened the principal, and sure enough the little boy found himself out on the street.

He was walking home in tears when a kindly woman came up and asked him what was wrong.

"Nobody wants to believe me," sobbed the little boy, "but my name is Osborne Green."

"Well, honey," said the woman, "I kin see the problem, 'cause I's born b-l-a-c-k."

•

What did George Washington and Thomas Jefferson have in common?

They were the last white people to have these names.

•

- Heard about the new toy store in Harlem?

It's called We Be Toys.

•

How come you never see a black family portrait?

Because when the photographer says, "Cheese," they all get in a straight line.

•

Three young black boys were taking a walk in a white neighborhood when they looked in a picture window and saw a couple making love on the couch. A policeman saw them peeking and hauled them into court.

"One of you boys come up here and tell me what was so interesting to look at," instructed the judge.

The first boy came up and reported, "I seen a white man on top of a white woman and they was fuckin'!"

"I fine you ten dollars for abusive language in the courtroom," boomed the judge. "Pay on the way out. You there, tell me what you saw."

The second boy came up and said, "I seen a white man on top of a white woman and they was fuckin'!"

Thoroughly irritated, the judge ordered him to pay the fine on the way out and turned to the third offender. "I suppose you're going to say the same thing?"

The boy shook his head.

"Well, what *did* you see?" asked the judge.

"I seen ten toes up and ten toes down, two white asses rollin' round and round, dick goin' out and dick goin' in, and if that ain't fuckin', you can fine me ten!"

•

Why did the black man pour Clearasil down his pants?

He wanted to get rid of a black head.

•

What do you call a traffic jam in Watts?

A blood clot.

•

A little black boy was busy playing in the backyard and ignored his mother's call to come in the house. In a few minutes she hollered again, "Ernie, you get in here *now.*"

The little boy kept on playing.

Finally his mother yelled, "Ernie, get your motherfucking ass in here!"

"Mama, don't call me a motherfucker," called back Ernie. "I ain't no motherfucker."

"You ain't in here yet neither," she answered.

•

Did you hear about the sequel to *Shogun* with an all-black cast?

It's going to be called *Shonuff*.

•

What do you call a black man's penis when it's not erect?

A jump rope.

•

To keep his costs down, Farmer Brown bought some robots to work his fields. Profits were increasing nicely when he received a visit from a representative of the State Highway Commission. Apparently the sunlight reflecting off the robots was disturbing westbound motorists on the nearby interstate.

"No problem," said Farmer Brown agreeably, and overnight he painted all the robots black.

The next morning only two showed up for work.

•

Why is a pussy like a black woman?

They both have big lips, kinky hair, and smell an hour after you wash them.

•

Heard the black answer to, "How many white folk do it take to screw in a lightbulb?"

"One, 'cause dey know how."

•

What's the difference between a pothole and a black?

You'd swerve to avoid a pothole.

•

Why did GM recall its latest-model Eldorados?

A watermelon won't fit in the glove compartment.

•

Do you know the five brands of automobiles named after blacks?

The Coontinental, the Jiguar, the Falcoon, the Cooneville, and the Poontang.

ETHNIC VARIEGATED

How do you bury a Greek?
  Flush.

·

How do you kill two Greeks with one shot?
  A shot in the ass of the one bending over.

·

What do Greeks wear to weddings?
  Formal fishnet.

·

A Pole, a Frenchman, and an American went deer hunting.
When the Frenchman came back to camp with a big buck,
his companions asked how he'd managed it. "I saw ze
tracks. I followed ze tracks. *Bang!* I got ze deer," was the
answer.

The next day it was the American who dragged a big buck back to camp. "I saw tracks, I followed 'em, and—*bang!*—I got the deer," was the story he told.

The third evening the Pole dragged himself into the camp, a bruised and bloody mess. "What the hell happened to you?" asked the other hunters.

"I saw the tracks. I followed the tracks, and—*bang!*" moaned the Pole, "I got hit by a train."

•

What's a Puerto Rican limousine?

A garbage truck with Mercedes hubcaps.

•

How about a Puerto Rican safari?

Three roaches and a can of Raid.

•

The nationwide limerick contest was drawing to a close, and the two finalists were Professor Keenan O'Hare from Boston, Massachusetts, and Big Leroy from Skeeterville, Mississippi. For the final competition, each finalist was given one minute in which to compose a limerick containing the word "Timbuktu." Professor O'Hare went first. After one minute he emerged, cleared his throat modestly, and recited:

> "Far away in a distant land
> Out across the burning sand
> Men on camels marched two by two
> On their way to Timbuktu."

The crowd applauded wildly, considering it a masterful piece of verse.

Then the judges set the timer for Leroy, who emerged

from the soundproof booth with a big grin on his face after only twenty seconds. He recited:

> "Me and my oldest brudda, Tim
> A huntin' we did go.
> We come upon three pretty gals
> A-sleepin' in a row.
> Since they was three and we was two
> I bucked one and Timbuktu."

•

Why don't Italians need to wear life preservers?
  Because oil floats.

•

Three men were trapped in the loft of a burning barn, and it soon became evident that the only way out was by jumping into a pile of horseshit. The American jumped first, and the manure only came up to his knees. The Frenchman was the next to jump, and it only came up to his waist. The Irishman jumped last, and the shit came all the way up to his neck. Know why?
  He jumped head first.

•

What's this. [Hold out your hand with the tip of your index finger touching the tip of your thumb to form a circle.]
  An Ethiopian stranglehold.

•

Once there was a penny-pinching farmer who decided to see if there was anyone out there gullible enough to rent his outhouse. So he put an ad in the paper, and within two weeks a nice Mexican family had set up house.

The rent came in regularly, and after a few months the farmer decided to take a stroll and see how his tenants were coming along. He was startled to see a couple of TV antennas sticking up from the roof.

"Oh, those," explained the Mexican father. "We rented out the basement to a couple of niggers."

•

What do you call an Italian prostitute?
Lasagne. (Lays on ya.)

•

How about a Hungarian prostitute?
Pig in a blanket.

•

Following a tragic shipwreck in the Mediterranean, the body of an attractive young woman was washed up on the beach near St. Tropez. The gendarme who came across it during his rounds went off to contact the coroner's office, and when he came back he was horrified to find his best friend on top of the corpse, going at it as hard as he could.

"Pierre, Pierre!" shouted the gendarme. "That woman . . . she is dead!"

"Dead!" howled Pierre, jumping up. "Sacre bleu—I took her for an American!"

•

An Englishman, a Frenchman, and an American were captured by Indians and taken back to their camp, where it soon became apparent that they were to receive no mercy. The Indian chief did, however, offer them the weapon of their choice with which to kill themselves.

"A pistol," requested the Englishman. "God Bless the

Queen," he pronounced, then blew his brains out. His companions watched in horror as the Indians flayed him and proceeded to make his skin into a canoe.

"Next?" inquired the chief.

The Frenchman asked for a sabre. "Vive la France," he gasped as he disemboweled himself and sank to the ground. The remaining captive again watched as the corpse was skinned and made into a canoe.

"And you, Yankee?" asked the chief.

"A fork," demanded the American. Grasping it with both hands, he proceeded to stab himself wildly, shrieking, "So much for your fucking canoe!"

•

How many Italians does it take to screw in a light bulb?

Two. One to screw it in and one to shoot the witnesses.

•

What's a WASP's idea of mass transit?

The ferry to Martha's Vineyard.

•

Sergei happened to run across his old friend Petya in Red Square. "Say," he whispered, "did you hear that Lermontov died?"

"You don't say!" exclaimed Petya. "And I didn't even know he'd been arrested."

•

What's a cannibal's favorite religious text?

"How to Serve Your Fellow Man."

•

What do you call a Chinese virgin?
  Too Young To.

•

How do you get twenty Argentinians in a phone booth?
  Let them think they own it.

•

What did the cannibals who caught a politician have for dinner?
  Baloney sandwiches.

•

Two Italians are walking down the street when one turns to the other and says, "Nunzio, you know, there's-a one time I really like to have-a sex."
  "When is-a that, Mario?" asked his friend.
  "Jus' before I have-a cigaretta."

•

Just before dawn an Indian chief walked into his daughter's tent unannounced, only to find her in an embrace with one of the village's handsome young braves. Irate, he said to the brave, "Now that you've had relations with my daughter, you must marry her. But first you must pass an endurance test to prove your worth."
  "I love your daughter," the young tribesman avowed, "and will be happy to submit to any test."
  The chief and the brave, wrapped in their bearskins because it was mid-February and five degrees below zero, walked down to the lake by the village. They stopped on the edge of the frozen lake and the chief said, "You must chop a hole in the ice, swim the three miles to the other side, then swim back. Upon your return, we shall have a great feast and you shall wed my daughter."

"Love shall sustain me through this trial of my manhood," the brave vowed. And when he had finished chopping through the ice, he plunged into the icy waters. Three hours later there was still no sign of him. And though the vigil was kept until the wee hours of the evening, by then, everyone in the village knew the worst—the young brave had not survived.

In his memory the chief's daughter decided to name the lake after her lover. And to this day, it's referred to as . . . Lake Stupid.

•

Hear about the guy who was half Jewish and half Japanese?
    He was circumcised at Benny Hannah's.

•

What do you call a Puerto Rican with no kids?
    A virgin.

•

While traveling across America by train, an Italian starts up a conversation with an attractive young woman dressed in faded blue jeans and loose blouse sitting in the seat next to him. *"Buena sera, signorina,"* he begins hopefully. "My name isa Giuseppe, and theese isa first time ina youra country." Answered by a smile, he goes on, "Whatsa your name, please, signorina?"

"Tee-hee," she giggled. "My name's Virginia—wanna fuck?"

Somewhat taken aback, but having read that the women in America were far more liberated than those back home, Giuseppe wastes no time in escorting Virginia back to his compartment, where they proceed to screw like crazy.

All of a sudden, the conductor's voice comes booming over the loudspeaker: "Camden, Baltimore, and Norfolk, Virginia!"

29

Amazed, the poor Italian looks up at the speaker and says, "Howa he know what I'ma do?"

•

What's a Greek tragedy?
Hemorrhoids.

•

What do you do with a dead Irishman who's too big for his coffin?
Give him an enema and stick him in a shoe box.

•

What do you call a skinny Protestant?
A Wisp.

•

Two Irishmen were trying to navigate through the Florida Everglades in a small boat when, all of a sudden, a huge alligator appeared by the side of the skiff and snapped its jaw at them a couple of times.

"Faith 'n' begorra, McCarthy!" screamed a frightened Murphy. "Did you take a look at that monster? It could gobble us both up in a second!"

"Fiddlesticks, you big sissy. Watch this." McCarthy laughed as he pulled down his pants and put his pecker right in the alligator's open mouth. Ten seconds later he removed his dick just before the reptile slammed its jaws shut.

"Holy Mother o' God! How did you be doing that?" asked an amazed Murphy.

"Oh, it was nothing," bragged McCarthy. "Why don't you try it?"

"I'd like to, McCarthy, me friend, but I don't think I could open me mouth that wide."

•

Why are Vietnamese like bananas?

They're green when they're put on the boat, perfectly good midway, and rotten when the come off.

•

How can you tell when a female WASP is experiencing an orgasm?

She uncrosses her legs.

•

Hear about the Japanese businessman who fell into a cesspool but couldn't swim?

He went through all the movements.

•

An Indian brave who had just married one of the village maidens walked into a pharmacy and said he needed a reliable condom for his wedding night. The next day, an upset Indian went back to the drugstore and told the pharmacist, "Squaw go oohh, me go aahh, rubber go ka-pooie."

"I'm so sorry," apologized the pharmacist. "Here, try this model. The rubber is of much stronger quality."

Bright and early the next morning, an irate Indian brave stormed into the pharmacy and yelled, "Squaw go oohh, me go aahh, rubber go ka-pooie!"

"Oh, my," muttered the druggist. "Okay, this prophylactic is made with the finest rubber. In fact, it's made of the same material as the Michelin radial tire. It's guaranteed to work."

A dejected Indian shuffled into the pharmacy the next morning, stopped in front of the pharmacist and sighed.

"Oh, no! Not again?" asked the amazed druggist.

Slowly the Indian shook his head and said, "Me go aahh, rubber go oohh, squaw go ka-pooie."

•

Did you know that having sex with an Arab is like poetry in motion?

Salaam, bam, thank you, ma'am.

•

Why did God create armadillos?

So Mexicans would have something to eat on the half-shell.

•

A Jew, an Irishman, and a Frenchman all died and went to heaven, where they were met at the Pearly Gates by Moses. He was looking through a large tome that outlined each man's life on earth.

"Hmmm, it says here that you loved money so much, you named your wife Penny," Moses said to the Jew as he leafed through the pages. "I'm sorry, but I have to send you to Hell."

Poof—the Jew disappeared.

"Let's see. Ahh, here it is," Moses declared, going on through the book. "Mr McNamara, you loved liquor so much, you called your wife Sherry. I'm sorry, you're going to have to join Mr. Cohen."

Poof—the Irishman disappeared.

"Mon dieu!" moaned the Frenchman. "Doun't waste your tim, Monsieur Moses. I had, how you say, bettre go weet zem—I called my wif Fanny!"

•

What do you get when you cross an Italian with a boar?

A guinea pig.

•

What do an Irishman and a houseplant have in common?
  They both die if they're not potted.

●

Why was the Irishman rushed to the hospital?
  He tried to drink a ship in a bottle.

●

What do you have when ten boat people go over a cliff in a Lincoln Continental?
  A damn shame—you can fit ten of them in a Hyundai.

●

What's black and weighs forty pounds?
  An Ethiopian.

●

What does an Ethiopian woman never say to her husband?
  "Eat me."

●

It so happened that Myron and Vinnie came of age at the same time. From his father Vinnie received a brand-new handgun, while at his bar mitzvah on the other side of town, Myron's father strapped a beautiful gold watch on his wrist. The next day after school Vinnie was full of admiration for the watch, while Myron was consumed with envy after one glance at the pistol. So the two friends decided to trade gifts.

That night when Vinnie checked to see whether it was dinnertime, his father asked, "Where'd you get thatta watch?" And on hearing the story, he exploded. "Whatsa matter you? Here I am t'inkin' you gotta some brains in your head. . ."

Vinnie looked frankly confused, so his father explained that some day Vinnie would probably get married. "An' somma day," he went on, "yous gonna find her in bed wit' another guy. An' whatta you gonna do then—look atta you watch and say, 'How long you gonna be?'"

•

Two cowboys came across an Indian lying with his ear to the ground. "See that Indian?" one cowboy asked the other.

"Yup."

"He's listening to the ground. He can hear anyone coming from miles away."

"You're shitting me," said the other cowboy, but just then the Indian looked up with an apprehensive expression.

"Covered wagon," the redskin reported, "about two miles away. Two oxen pulling husband and wife and three noisy children, plus all household belongings."

"Incredible!" admitted the skeptical cowboy. "How does he know not only how far away the wagon is, but what's *in* it?"

The Indian lifted his head again. "Ran me over about forty minutes ago."

•

What do you call a Norwegian car?

A Fjord.

•

Upper-class Brit: "I'm terribly sorry to hear that you buried your wife today."

Even-more-Upper-class Brit: "Had to. Dead, you know."

•

Two Swedish sailors disembark in some sleazy little seaport and head for the nearest bar. Each orders a whiskey, downs

34

it in a gulp, orders another, downs it, and in short order orders, puts away a third, fourth, and fifth drink. At this point Olaf orders yet another round, turns to his companion, and says, "Skoal!"

"Hey," returns the other Swede belligerently, "did you come here to bullshit or did you come here to drink?"

•

What's the difference between a Jew and a black?
   About 3,600 years.

•

How about the difference between a black and a Hispanic?
   About ten minutes in the oven.

•

What was the WASP national anthem of the 1960s?
   "O, Canada!"

•

What's a Puerto Rican car pool?
   Thirty of them in a Honda Civic.

•

A Pole, a Jew, and a German came to their last days on death row, and the prison officials gave them a choice of electrocution, hanging, or death by Big Bertha. The Jew chose electrocution. A few minutes later a light flashed across the corridor, and the Jew was dead. The German chose hanging, and when a *snap!* was heard down the corridor, they knew he was dead.

The Pole opted for Big Bertha and was led down the hall and into a large room. As the door clanged shut behind him, he saw a humongous fat lady standing there. "Tighten my belt," she instructed the Pole. "Now stick one hand up my pussy," she ordered. "Now, loosen my belt." And—*skllorp!*—the Pole disappeared.

*

Do you know why Irish dogs have snubbed noses?
  From chasing parked cars.

*

What's the best-selling deodorant in Puerto Rico?
  Raid.

*

How come Irish women don't give good head?
  They can't get their lips past his ears.

*

What's a "wiener"?
  The first runner to cross the finish line in a Mexican track meet.

*

Let's hear it for Down Under:

If you could get some Jews to wander in the desert for forty years by dropping a nickel, what would it take to get twenty million Australians to do the same?
  A case of beer buried in the same desert.

*

Hear that the Australians have replaced "God Save the Queen" with a new national anthem?

It goes, "A hundred bottles of beer on the wall, a hundred bottles of beer . . ."

•

In Britain they have the House of Lords and the House of Commons—
In Australia they have a brothel and a garbage can.

•

What do you call an Australian with an IQ of twenty?
Tasmanian.

And with an IQ above one hundred?
An aborigine.

•

They have a new poster out to build Australian pride.
It says: Australia—Land of Strong Men (and Nervous Sheep)

•

What's a Tasmanian devil?
An Australian in heat.

•

And from a bumper sticker:
WESTERN AUSTRALIA, WE'RE DOING IT! (WITH SHEEP)

•

A little song from Mexico:
My name is Fernando,
I come from the lando,

I make three dollars a day.
I take it to Lucy,
Who gives me some pussy,
And takes my two dollars away!"

•

How can you spot the Irishman in a department store?
  He's the one caught in the revolving door.

•

How come Pakistanis go around with their flies open?
  In case they have to count to eleven.

•

Why don't WASPs approve of artificial insemination?
  They don't like the idea of using someone else's leftovers.

•

Three addicts went into a favorite back alley to shoot up.
The black addict sterilized his needle, swabbed it with alcohol, and shot up. Then he passed it to the Jewish addict, who sterilized it, swabbed it with alcohol, and shot up. Then he passed it to the Polish addict, who stuck the needle right in his arm.
  "Are you crazy, man?" screamed the first two. "Haven't you heard of AIDS? You could get sick, man, you could *die*."
  "Don't be ridiculous," said the Polish addict in a lofty tone. "I'm wearing a condom."

•

What's furry and generates enough steam to melt an iceberg?
  An Eskimo in heat.

•

Abdul, Ali, and Hassan were riding across the Sahara when their way was blocked by a large sand dune. Ali rode around to the right, Hassan cut to the left, but stubborn Abdul forced his camel to ride straight through it.

On the other side two camels were making love, and Abdul popped out of the dune at the very moment of orgasm. Startled, the camels pulled apart, and Abdul was showered with camel come.

Fifteen minutes later, Ali and Hassan finally arrive on the other side of the dune. Seeing their dripping friend trying to dry himself off, Ali whispered to Hassan, "Poor Abdul—he just doesn't know enough to rein in out of the come."

•

What's a fart?
  A Greek love call.

•

What's an Irish seven-course dinner?
  A six-pack and a boiled potato.

•

How do Italians count to ten?
  One, two, three, another, another, another . . ."

•

A Jew, a Russian, and a black were driving cross-country in a truck when it broke down in rural Iowa. So they walked down the road to the nearest farmhouse and received permission to sleep in the shed. "Just don't mess with my daughter," admonished the farmer.

In the middle of the night the Jew announced he had to take a leak, went out, and screwed the farmer's daughter. He hadn't been back in bed very long when the Russian announced the same urge, went out, and screwed the farmer's daughter. Just before dawn the black, too, had screwed the farmer's daughter.

When the three got up in the morning, the farmer was standing in front of the shed with a shotgun. "You sons of bitches fooled with my little Nancy, didn't you?" he said accusingly, and his guests admitted they had.

"See that fence over there?" asked the farmer, gesturing with his shotgun. "I'll give you thirty seconds to jump it, cross the field, run through the mud, jump that far fence, and screw a cow in the pasture before I shoot you like a dog."

The Russian took to his heels, scrambling over the fence and through the mud before his time was up and the farmer shot him. Next went the black, who made it over the far fence before the farmer's bullet brought him down. The panicked Jew fell to his knees, but the farmer told him to get moving unless he wanted to get shot then and there. So the Jew sprinted over the fence, across the field, through the mud, over the second fence, and fucked a cow, all before his time was up.

"Not bad," conceded the farmer, shaking his head admiringly. "I reckon you're man enough to marry my daughter."

"The hell with your daughter," retorted the Jew. "How much do you want for the cow?"

•

What do you get when you cross a WASP and a Mexican?
    A migrant stockbroker.

•

What do Japanese men do when they have erections?
    Vote.

•

What did the Mexican guy and the Polish girl name their baby?

Retardo.

•

The harbor cruise boat was returning to the dock after a cruise around Sydney Harbor with a group of Japanese tourists aboard. One young man was in such a hurry to get back on land and continue sightseeing that he jumped from the deck before the gangplank was in place. Unfortunately he lost his footing and was crushed between the boat and the pier. "Look at that crab," remarked the captain to a member of the crew.

"Crab?" queried the puzzled sailor. "That's a man, sir, one of those Japanese fellows."

"That's what I mean by crab," explained the captain. "A crushed-Asian."

•

What's the difference between an Italian and a Pole pissing in the sink?

The Pole takes the dishes out first.

•

Hear about the new synagogue in Harlem?

It's called Temple Beth-You-Is-My-Woman-Now.

•

What do you get when you cross an Italian with a Pole?

A hitman who misses.

•

What are the first four words a Puerto Rican child learns?

"Give me your money!"

HOMOSEXUAL

What's a chastity belt for homosexuals?
  An anal suppository.

•

While hitchhiking across country, a young dyke hailed a ride from a car driven by a beautiful woman who also happened to be gay. A few hours later, the driver asked her passenger if she'd mind if they stopped at a motel for a couple of hours so she could get some rest. The rider said she was tired too and suggested they share a room to save money. That evening, as they both lay in the same double bed, the hitchhiker gently put her hand on the other woman's arm and said, "Let me be frank . . ."

  "No, no, please," protested the other woman, "let me be Frank. You can be Bob."

•

Hear about the two faggot judges?
　They wanted to try each other.

•

How are gays brought into this world?
　They're sucked into it.

•

Why did the boy refuse to live with his gay uncle?
　He didn't want to be reared by a faggot.

•

Hear what happened to the homosexual with amnesia?
　He lost his ball bearings.

•

What do you call a group of homosexual musicians?
　Band-AIDS.

•

What's the gay scoutmaster's motto?
　"Out of every young scout, a mature man will emerge."

•

Did you hear about the new lesbian sneakers?
　They were called Dykies. But they were recalled because
the tongues weren't long enough.

•

What do you feed gay babies?
　Spermilac.

•

What's the Phone Sex company's motto?

"Reach out and suck someone."

•

The cabbie struck up a casual conversation with his passenger, who suddenly asked, "Say, if you woke up in the morning and found Vaseline on your asshole, would you tell anyone?"

"Gee . . ." answered the startled cabbie, "No, I don't think I would."

"Great!" said the passenger. "Would you go camping with me?"

•

Two gays had gotten bored with their nightly routine, so Maurice took it into his head to go down to the butcher shop and purchase a big piece of sausage. He picked out a piece of appropriate dimensions and asked the butcher to wrap it up. But to his considerable dismay, when he got the package he realized the butcher had sliced the sausage up into pieces the size of quarters.

"Goddamn it!" snapped the irate fag. "Does he think my asshole's a slot machine?"

•

What's the difference between a hobo and a homo?

A hobo has no friends at all, whereas a homo has friends up the ass.

•

The CIA burst into a dingy hotel room in Lisbon to find their worst suspicions confirmed: there was the station chief locked in a homosexual embrace with a known Soviet spy. Jumping to his feet, the Soviet threw himself melodramatically in front of the agents.

"Shoot if you must this old gay red,
But spare your country's fag," he said.

•

Why didn't the gay legislator ask for help in drafting the tax bill?
He had Congressional AIDS.

•

What does a gay candy maker do?
Packs fudge.

•

A gay man was standing in front of his mirror brushing his teeth when his gums started to bleed. "Thank God," he said to himself. "Safe for another month."

•

The whaling vessel had been at sea for many months when the troubled mate paid a visit to the captain's cabin. "I think there is unnatural sex going on aboard this ship, Captain," he summarily informed him. The captain told him to come back when he had proof and dismissed him.

A few days later the mate came forward with the same accusation and again the captain brushed off the charges, telling him to come back when he could furnish some evidence. So he was rather startled when the empty-handed mate came to speak to him a third time.

"I must insist on proof," he reprimanded the sailor.

"But, Captain," blurted the mate unhappily, "this is the third time I've tasted shit on Matthew Smith's prick!"

•

What did one lesbian say to the girl she'd just met at the gay bar?

"Like to come back to my place for some twat-tails?"

•

Heard about the new convenience food that's selling like crazy in Greenwich Village?

It's called Semen Helper.

•

What's the sexist definition of a lesbian?

Just another damn woman trying to do a man's job.

•

How do you pick up a quarter on Polk Street?

Kick it to Van Ness.

•

One day Sam screwed up his courage and went to see a therapist, telling him he thought he was gay. "And what makes you think that?" queried the doctor.

"Well," answered Sam, "my grandfather was gay."

The therapist explained that sexual preference was not thought to be a hereditary trait.

"Okay," Sam went on, "but my father was gay too."

"That's certainly unusual," conceded the doctor, "but it doesn't make you a homosexual."

"Yeah, but then there's my brother."

"He's gay too?" exclaimed the doctor. "Doesn't anyone in your family sleep with women?"

"Of course," replied Sam. "My sister."

•

What's the difference between a gay rodeo and a straight rodeo?

At a straight rodeo they yell, "Ride that sucker!"

CELEBRITY

Hear what they found when they took Tammy Bakker's makeup off?
  Jimmy Hoffa.

*

What does PTL stand for?
  Part Thy Legs or Pay The Lady.

*

What do Vale, Colorado, and Tammy Bakker have in common?
  A good foundation and ten inches of powder.

*

What does LORD stand for?
  Let Oral Roberts Die.

*

Why was Catherine Parr down on King Henry the VIII?
  She thought all rulers had twelve inches.

•

How did Sylvester Stallone get AIDS?
  He was in Rocky too.

•

What do you get when you cross a Cabbage Patch Doll with the Pillsbury Doughboy?
  A bitch with a yeast infection.

•

One cold winter day the Lone Ranger and Tonto were riding across the prairie. Tonto stopped his horse, got off, and put his ear to the ground. A few minutes later he spoke up: "Buffalo come."
  "Amazing," said the Lone Ranger. "How do you know?"
  "Ear stuck to ground."

•

The bum chose matinee time, when the streets of the theater district were crowded with people hurrying to get to the show, to do his panhandling. Sizing up a well-dressed gentleman, he lurched over and asked politely, "Sir, may I borrow a quarter?"
  The well-heeled man looked over the top of his glasses at the bum, cleared his throat, and quoted, "'Neither a borrower nor a lender be'—William Shakespeare."
  The bum looked back at him and retorted, "'Up yours, cocksucker'—David Mamet."

•

What do Lassie and Halley's comet have in common?
  Both are stars with tails.

•

Why did Dolly Parton's teeth fall out?
  Her dentist couldn't reach them.

•

Did you hear about the Ayatollah Khomeini doll?
  Wind it up and it takes Barbie and Ken hostage.

•

When does the Jolly Green Giant go "Ho, ho, ho?"
  When someone plays with his little green sprout.

•

Know why Frankenstein can't get laid?
  His nuts are in his neck.

•

Hear what Richard Nixon said about his latest sexual experience?
  "What a wonderful encounter. I just wish there had been someone to enjoy it with."

•

What do you call a person holding a large green ball in each hand?
  Someone with the Jolly Green Giant's complete attention.

•

Four presidents were relaxing after the summit meeting and talking about the finest things their countries had to offer.

"We have the best looking mountains in the vorld," declared the German president, rising to his feet.

The French president rose and said, "My country, she has the greenest grass of ze whole world."

The Mexican president stood up and pronounced, "In Mexico we have the bes' flag in the world."

"Well, as a matter of fact," pondered Reagan, as he sat up in his chair, realizing that this was a perfect opportunity to demonstrate his political acumen, "we have the best eagle, because it can fly over your mountains, shit on your grass, and wipe his ass on your flag."

•

What was the scandal that forced Gary Hart out of the presidential campaign called?

Tailgate.

•

Did you know Hart placed a long-distance call during that weekend in Bimini?

He said, "I've got her in the water, Ted—now what do I do?"

•

And what did Donna Rice and Christie McAuliffe have in common?

They both went down on the challenger.

•

What do Gary Hart and the Japan's prime minister, Yasuhiro Nakasone, have in common?

They both eat rice.

•

Richard Nixon, Gary Hart, and Ted Kennedy are planning on starting a new law firm together. Know what they're going to call it?

Trick 'em, Lick 'em, and Dunk 'em.

○

Know what Donna Rice and the Democratic primary party have in common?

Gary Hart pulled out of both of them.

○

Let us not forget Senator Ted,
Who took a young woman to bed.
He said, "It's no-uuh-crime
To have a good time."
But yet, the young woman is dead.

○

"How do you feel about having been born blind?" a sympathetic reporter asked Stevie Wonder.

"It could've been worse," answered the singer philosophically. "I could've been born black!"

○

What's the difference between Joan Rivers and a whoopee cushion?

A whoopee cushion is funny.

○

How come they had to keep turning Karen Anne Quinlan before she finally died?

Moss kept growing on her north side.

○

What did Yoko say when she heard John had been shot?
  "Oh, no!"

•

Know what kind of contraceptive the fashion conscious man is wearing these days?
  Brooke Shields.

•

What do Pete Rose and the Mafia have in common?
  Three thousand hits.

•

What vegetable won't be served at dinner any more in Newport?
  Sunny Von Bulow.

•

What's black and white and has three eyes?
  Sammy Davis, Jr. and his wife.

HANDICAPPED

What do promiscuous angels get?
  Harpies.

•

What's Helen Keller's idea of oral sex?
  A manicure.

•

What two words do blind men hear most often?
  "Wrong hole!"

•

The new bus driver for the Sesame Street Elementary School for Exceptional Children was a bit nervous his first day on the job. Clutching the map and the list of names he'd been provided with, the driver made his way to the first stop, where a very fat little girl boarded the bus. "Hi," she said, "My name is Patty." The driver tried to return her smile as she took a seat.

At the next stop, an extremely fat little girl got on. The driver managed a weak smile when she said, "Hi, my name's Patty," and waddled to a seat.

Next was a little boy sporting thick glasses, crutches, and a safety helmet. His list informed the driver that this was "Special" Ross, and he helped the little boy up the stairs and into a seat.

The last child to be picked up was a boy named Lester T., and to the driver's relief he appeared perfectly normal. Accelerating, he was near the school when a strange smell came over the bus. Looking in his rearview mirror, the driver saw that Lester had his socks and shoes off and was picking at bunions on his feet. Totally grossed out, the driver lost control of the bus and crashed into a guard rail.

The police were quickly on the scene. Ascertaining that no one had been hurt, they turned to the bus driver and asked what the hell had come over him.

"Well, wouldn't *you* go crazy?" asked the bus driver indignantly. "It's not even 9:00 and I've had two obese Pattys, Special Ross, Lester T. picking bunions on a Sesame Street bus!"

•

What's the worst favor you can ask of a leper?

To lend you a hand.

•

Graffiti in the men's room:
DYSLEXICS, UNTIE!

•

Which doesn't belong with the rest: AIDS, herpes, gonorrhea, condominiums?

Gonorrhea. You can get rid of gonorrhea.

•

Did you hear about the poor baby born without an eyelid? In order to do a transplant, the doctor first performed a circumcision so he could fashion an eyelid from the foreskin. Both operations went perfectly, except for one small problem: the doctor's afraid the baby's going to be a *little* cockeyed.

•

How did Helen Keller pierce her ear?
    Answering the stapler.

•

And how do you torture Helen Keller?
    Turn her clothing inside out.

•

Two carrots were standing by the edge of the road when a roadster came around the bend and hit one of them. The next day the carrot visited his friend in the hospital. "What do you think, Doc?" he asked, spotting him down the hallway.

"He'll recover," the doctor reassured him, "but, frankly, he'll be a vegetable for the rest of his life."

CRUELTY TO ANIMALS

Why did the chicken cross the road?
  Kentucky Fried Chicken was there—and they do chicken right!

•

Why don't male alligators in the Okefenokee Swamp have sex?
  They're afraid they'll get gatoraids.

•

A duck went into a drugstore and asked for a condom.
  "Cash?" asked the clerk.
  "No," said the duck, "just put it on my bill."

•

Which came first, the chicken or the egg?
  The chicken. The egg just got laid.

•

What's smaller than a teeny-weeny flea?
    A flea's teeny weenie.

•

Remember what's red and green and goes 100 mph?
    A frog in a blender.
So what do you get if you add milk?
    Frog nog.

•

What do you get when you cross a rooster with a pack of Chewels?
    A cock that goes squirt.

•

And when you cross a rooster with a lollipop?
    A cocksucker.

•

Why did the farmer name the unwanted puppies Un, Deux, Trois, and Quatre?
    Because when he threw them in the lake, Un, Deux, Trois, and Quatre sank.

•

What do you call a calf's pussy?
    Veal cuntlet.

•

What do you call it when a chicken cheats at cards?
    Foul play.

•

What do you get when you cross a tortoise with a cow?
  A turtleneck jersey.

•

If there were three elephants in your kitchen, which would
be the cowboy?
  The one on the range.

•

Why do elephants drink?
  It helps them forget.

•

Why can't elephants fly on airplanes?
  Because they can't fit their trunks under the seats.

•

How can you tell if an elephant has been in your refrigerator?
  Footprints in the butter.

•

Why do hummingbirds hum?
  They don't know the words.

•

What's green and leaps into bed?
  A prostitoad.

•

What did the woman say to the centipede running across her chest?

"No, no, a thousand times no!"

•

How much did the psychiatrist charge the elephant?

$385. $35 for the visit and $350 for the sofa.

•

What do you get when you cross a cat with a lemon?

A sourpuss.

•

A man with a poodle went into a bar, ordered a drink and asked for a pack of Marlboros. The bartender told the man he was sorry, but that he had just run out of cigarettes. "Don't worry about it," reassured the man. "I'll just send my dog across the street for some."

Going through his pockets, the man realized he only had a twenty-dollar bill. "Pack of Marlboros, pal," he said, putting the bill in the dog's mouth, "and I want to see plenty of change." The dog jumped down from the barstool and ran out the door.

"That dog is something else," said an admiring customer. "Is he really going to bring you back a pack of cigarettes?"

"You bet. My dog can do just about anything—" But his list of the poodle's accomplishments was interrupted by the screech of tires outside the bar. Turning pale, the man ran outside and to his relief saw that the car had missed his pet. The reason for the sudden halt, however, was obvious. Right in the middle of the street his poodle was busy humping another dog.

"What's going on?" asked the man, running up to his dog. "You never did anything like this before!"

Humping away, the dog looked up and said, "I never had twenty bucks before!"

•

What do female hippos say before sex?
   "Can I be on top this time?"

•

Confucius say, "As one goes through life, it is better to be like the dog—if it cannot be eaten or made love to, then piss on it."

•

Two worms shared a nice hole underneath a golf course. "Go up and see if it's raining," demanded Ernie one morning.

   "Why should I be the one to get all wet?" protested Duane. They yelled back and forth until the argument was settled by drawing straws, and Duane reluctantly headed up the hole.

   Just at this moment two women golfers passed overhead, one complaining about how badly she had to pee. "There's nobody around," said her partner. "Why don't you do it right here?" So the woman squatted down and started to pee, just as Duane stuck his head up above the surface. Drenched by the torrent of urine, Duane hurried back down the hole.

   "So I see it's raining," commented Ernie dryly.

   "Yeah," gasped Duane, reaching for a towel to wipe his face. "In fact it's raining so hard the birds are building their nests upside down."

•

The bartender was dumbfounded when a gorilla came in and asked for a martini, but he couldn't think of any reason not to serve the beast. And he was even more amazed to find the gorilla coolly holding out a ten-dollar bill when he returned with the drink.

As he walked over to the cash register, he decided to try something. He rang up the sale, headed back to the animal, and handed it a dollar in change. Nonplussed, the gorilla just sat there sipping his martini.

Finally the bartender couldn't take it anymore. "You know," he offered, "we don't get too many *gorillas* in here."

And the gorilla returned, "At nine bucks a drink, I'm not surprised."

•

Watching his dog carefully lick every bit of his cock and balls, Mr. Jones got so downright envious that he decided to strip, get down on the floor, and try it himself.

A few minutes later Mrs. Jones walked in. "I've heard of teaching old dogs new tricks," she sighed, "but this is ridiculous!"

•

At their annual football game the big animals are really trouncing the little animals with a tremendous offensive game. At halftime the score is 33–0, and it's only with considerable effort that the little animals manage to stop the opposition's kickoff return on the twenty-two-yard line. On the first down, the big animals send the hippopotamus around the right end, but as soon as he gets to the line of scrimmage—*bang!*—he's stopped cold.

Back in the huddle, the squirrel, captain of the little animals, says, "Say, that was great! Who stopped the hippo, anyway?"

"Me," said the centipede.

On the second down, the rhino charges around the left end, but he too is stopped cold at the line of scrimmage. "Terrific," cheers the squirrel. "Who did it this time?"

"Me," said the centipede.

On the third down the big animals send the elephant right up the middle, but he doesn't get one yard before he's knocked flat on his back. "Was that you again?" the squirrel asked the bug.

"Yup," said the centipede modestly.

"Well, where the hell were you during the first half?" demanded the captain.

"Taping my ankles."

.

Seen the new porno movie about animal sodomy?

It's called *Sheep Throat*.

.

What do you get when you cross an elephant with a prostitute?

A two-ton pickup.

.

Why do elephants have trunks in the first place?

Because they don't have glove compartments.

FEMALE

Define cunt.
  A root canal.

·

What do you call a man who goes around deflowering virgins?
  A fuzz buster.

·

What's a prostitute's favorite rock group?
  Yes.

·

What's black and hairy and fell off the wall?
  Humpty Cunt!

·

A famous Russian ballerina defected to the U.S., so there was considerable excitement on the opening night of her American premiere. Everything went along very smoothly before a very receptive audience, and finally it was time for the grand finale. The entire troupe swirled about the ballerina, who performed a final spectacular set of leaps and landed in a perfect split in center stage.

Needless to say, the crowd went wild, and it was only after a standing ovation and five curtain calls that the curtain closed for the last time. Rushing onstage to the ballerina, who was still holding the perfect split, the director began to congratulate her on her superb performance.

"Performance, hell," hissed the dancer. "Rock me back and forth to break the seal."

•

What's the difference between pussy and tit?
One gets dicked and one gets licked.

•

What noise do vinegar and water make when they collide?
Doooooooouuuche!

•

Leonard desperately wanted to become a doctor and had really crammed for his medical boards, so he wasn't in the least fazed by the question: Name the three advantages of breast milk.

Quickly he wrote, 1) It contains the optimum balance of nutrients for the newborn child. He added, 2) As it is contained within the mother's body, it is protected from germs and helps develop the child's immune system. Then Leonard was stumped. Sitting back and racking his brains until he'd broken into a sweat, he finally scribbled, 3) It comes in great containers!

•

Two law partners hire a gorgeous young receptionist, and despite promises to the contrary, neither can resist going to bed with her. And not too long afterward their worst fears are realized: the blushing receptionist announces that she's pregnant. No one knows who the father is, and the partners are in a total quandary. So toward the end of the pregnancy they decide to chip in and send the girl off to Florida to have the baby.

Several months go by with no news, and finally one of the partners feels so guilty that he hops on a flight to Miami to check on the young mother. The next night the phone rings in their New York office.

"How is she?" asks his partner.

"Oh, she's fine," was the breezy answer, "but I've got some bad news and some good news."

"Oh, yeah? What's the good news?"

"Well, like I said, Jeannette's fine. And she had twins."

"So what's the bad news?" asked the partner from New York.

"Mine died."

•

If whiskey makes you frisky and gin makes you grin, what makes you pregnant?

Two highballs and a squirt.

•

The voluptuous stewardess asked the dirty old man, "May I offer you some TWA soda, some TWA coffee, or some TWA milk?"

Winking lewdly, he suggested, "How about some TWA tea?"

•

The job of assistant at the general store had been taken over by a ripe, but none too bright, young girl with a penchant for short skirts. The local boys delighted in sending her on errands to the top shelves of the store because the view from underneath the ladder was most enticing.

One morning, noticing that all the raisin bread was stocked on an upper shelf, the guys were amusing themselves by sending the girl up the ladder again and again for the bread. An older man walked into the store and waited in line, quietly taking in the scene. Returning behind the counter with the last loaf of bread under her arm, she asked him, "Is yours raisin too?"

"No," he admitted, "but it's starting to twitch."

•

What do electric train sets and women's breasts have in common?

Both were intended for children, but it's the fathers who play with them.

•

What's harder than getting six pregnant women in a Volkswagen?

Getting six women pregnant in a Volkswagen.

•

The conductor was hard at work on his podium when he heard severe disharmony from the cello section. Stopping the orchestra, he glared at the woman cellist.

"My dear madam," he snapped, "you have a magnificent instrument between your legs. Must you stand there and simply scratch at it?"

•

Did you hear about the call girl who accidentally made two appointments at the same time?

She managed to squeeze both of them in.

•

What do you call a man and a woman using the rhythm method of birth control?

Parents.

•

What's a rib tickler?

A vibrator shoved in too far.

•

[You need to be holding something to drink when you tell this one.]

Knowing her fiancé was also a virgin, the night before the wedding the bride to be asked her mother about the mysteries of sex. Her mother was glad to oblige with some pointers.

That night, following all the festivities, the nervous husband took off his glasses and slid under the covers, but just looking at his pretty new wife gave him a massive hard-on. "I think I know what to do," she said, sizing up the situation, and proceeded to go down on him. After just a minute or two the fellow couldn't contain himself and blew his wad. As he raved about how fantastic it had felt, his wife got into her side of the bed, and almost immediately felt another hard-on against her thigh. Looking over at him, she proceeded to go down on him again. And, groaning with ecstasy, the husband blew his wad again.

"Oh, darling," he said kneeling beside the bed, "you've pleased me so very much. Is there anything I can do for you?"

[Now's when you ask, "What do you think she said?" and take a swallow in your mouth.]

[Spit out your drink.] "Kiss me."

•

What's the definition of eternity?

The length of time between when *you* come and *she* leaves.

•

John: Did you hear that report on the six-o'clock news about the old lady found with a rat in her stomach?
Ray: No. How'd it happen?
John: Her pussy fell asleep.

•

A female midget went to her gynecologist with the complaint that her crotch was hurting her. "When does the pain occur?" he asked.

"When it's raining out, oddly enough."

"Since I don't see anything amiss, why don't you come in the next time it hurts?" proposed the doctor.

The very next rainy day the midget limped into his office. "Doc, my crotch is killing me right now."

The doctor had her lie on the table in the examining room and put her feet in the stirrups. Covering her knees with a sheet, he reached for some surgical scissors and began to snip away. "That should do it," he reported, sitcking his head up after a few minutes.

Dressing and coming into his office, the woman exclaimed, "Doctor, the pain is completely gone! How did you do it?"

The doctor explained modestly, "Oh, I just cut two inches off the tops of your galoshes."

•

The new stewardess was summoned to the office of the head of the training program for a severe reprimand. "I heard about that episode on your first flight, Miss Larson," she said, glaring over the top of her glasses. "From now on, whenever a passenger feels faint, I'll thank you to push his head down between his own legs!"

•

What did the doctor say to the nymphomaniac?

"Take two aspirin and ball me in the morning."

•

As the woman in front of him stepped up into the bus, the man noticed that her skirt was stuck between the cheeks of her ass, so he reached up and pulled it free.

"How dare you!" yelped the woman, turning and slapping him in the face.

"Sorry, lady," said the man, and stuck it back in again.

•

Sam and Cindy grew up next door to each other and as they grew older each constantly tried to one-up the other. If Sam got a jungle gym, Cindy got a swing set, and so on, until the contest became a very expensive one for both sets of parents. Finally Sam's father asked what was going on, and when Sam explained it, a big grin came over his face.

Next Saturday Cindy whizzed down the sidewalk on a brand new tricycle. "Nyaah, nyaah," she taunted, "look what I've got."

"So?" retorted Sam. "I've got something you'll never have—look!" And he pulled down his pants and showed her.

Realizing she'd been outdone, Cindy ran into her house sobbing. Her father picked her up and tried to comfort her. Getting the whole story out of her, he smiled and whispered something in her ear.

The next day Sam spotted Cindy in the back yard and decided to rub it in. "I've got one of these and you don't," he teased, pulling his pants down again.

"Big deal," said Cindy hautily, pulling her skirt up and her underpants down. "My daddy says that with one of *these* I can have as many of *those* as I want."

•

What was Adam's first toy?
  Eve.

•

After Marty's and Mindy's marriage ended in a particularly bitter divorce, Mindy remarried within six months. Not long afterward she ran into her ex-husband at a local restaurant where she was having lunch with a girlfriend.

"So," said Marty, sidling up to their table, "how's your new husband?"

"Just fine, thanks," answered Mindy calmly.

"And how does he like your old, tired, worn-out pussy?" inquired Marty with a leer.

"Oh, he likes it just fine," Mindy said cheerfully, ". . . once he got past the old, worn-out part."

•

Drunk: Knock, knock.
Woman: Who's there?
Drunk: Emerson.
Woman: Emerson who?
Drunk: Emerson pretty big tits you got there!

•

What would be one of the best things about electing a woman for vice president?
  We wouldn't have to pay her as much!

•

What do a hooker and a shotgun have in common?
  One cock and they're ready to blow.

•

What do a hooker and a doorknob have in common?
Everybody gets a turn.

·

What do a hooker and a pie have in common?
Everybody gets a piece.

·

What do a hooker and railroad tracks have in common?
They're spread all over.

·

What do a hooker and an ice cream cone have in common?
Everybody gets a lick.

·

What do a hooker and a bus have in common?
Everybody pays to get on.

MALE ANATOMY

What did the stewardess say to the flasher?
"I asked for your ticket, not your stub."

•

What's the coldest part of an Eskimo?
His balls—because they're two below.

•

An hour after checking into the motel, the traveling sales-man stormed up to the front desk. "What kind of chicken-shit joint are you running?" he demanded.

"What's the problem, sir?" stammered the confused desk clerk.

"I went up to my room, unlocked the door, and there was a man holding a gun," blustered the irate guest. "He told me to get on my knees and give him a blow job or he'd blast my brains all over the room."

"Oh my God," gasped the clerk, shocked and embarrassed. "What did you do?"

The salesman screamed, "Well, you didn't hear any shots, did you?"

•

Walking along a deserted beach, a man finds an empty bottle that he picks up and rubs. Sure enough, a genie appears and offers the man two wishes.

"I wish I were always hard and could get all the ass I wanted," he informs the genie.

"Whatever turns you on," the genie replied and turned the man into a toilet seat.

•

When sixteen-year-old Gary came home with the news that he'd gotten laid for the first time, his mother was less than pleased. Slapping him across the face, she sent him off to his room without any supper. When Gary's father got home and heard the news, he went up to see his son.

"Well, Gary," he admonished, secretly pleased, "I hope you learned something from this experience."

"You bet I did," admitted his son. "Next time I use Vaseline. My ass is killing me!"

•

Why is a woman's blind date like a snowstorm?

She never knows how many inches she'll get or how long it will last.

•

"Hey, pal," the irate druggist shouted, "put that cigar out while you're in my store!"

"I bought this cigar here," complained the customer.

"Big deal," rejoined the druggist. "We sell condoms too."

•

A man out for his daily constitutional runs into a young girl who's crying her eyes out. "What's wrong?" he asked.

"Leroy's dead!" she wailed.

A few more blocks down the street, he comes across a group of women all weeping. "Leroy's dead!" they're moaning.

Continuing on his walk, he decides to stop in at the local funeral parlor and to ask the undertaker what all the fuss is about. Without saying a word, the undertaker pulls a sheet off the table next to him and exposes a naked body with a fourteen-inch cock.

"Is that Leroy?"

The undertaker nods.

"Hey, I'll give you fifty dollars for that guy's penis."

The undertaker nods.

Stuffing the dick in a paper bag, the fellow runs home to his wife, bounds up the stairs and shouts, "You're not going to believe what I've got in this bag."

The curious wife takes the bag from her husband, peeks inside, and screams, "Leroy's dead!"

•

A young boy, head hung in submission, sat across from a priest in the church confessional. "Forgive me, Father, for I have sinned," he lamented. "I've been having sex with some of the animals on our farm."

"Hmm," muttered the priest. "Were these animals male or female?"

"What the hell do you think I am," shouted the boy, "a faggot?"

•

A man taking a tour through hell with the devil sees a room filled with wine bottles and beautiful, naked women.

"I could have a good time in that room." He snickered.

"That's what you think," said the devil, winking slyly.

"See those wine bottles? They all have holes in the bottom. See those women? They don't!"

•

Hear about the young boy whose mother caught him jerking off in the bathroom?

She told him to stop because he'd go blind, and he asked if he could keep going till he needed glasses.

•

One night after work, Scott is greeted at the door by his wife clad in a flimsy negligee. Before he has a chance to remove his coat, she falls to her knees, yanks his fly down, pulls his dick out, and proceeds to give him a wonderful, sloppy blow job.

"All right!" Scott says. "What happened to the car?"

•

An unemployed porno star was looking for someone to represent him. "Do you have an eight-by-ten?" asked an agent.

"Shit," said the actor, "if I had an eight-by-ten, I wouldn't be out of work."

•

"Stop!" screams Nancy as her boyfriend fucks her up the ass. "It hurts!"

"You're crazy," Rambo replies. "It feels good!"

•

While in the midst of a passionate embrace with a prostitute, the admiral asks, "Well, how'm I doing, mate?"

"Oh, I'd say you're doing about three knots," the hooker answered.

"Arrgh, matey, what do you mean by three knots?" he queried with a leer.

"You're not hard, you're not in, and you're not getting a refund."

•

"Father," whispered the young man on the eve of his wedding, "what am I supposed to do? I'm a little nervous."

"Don't worry about a thing," consoled the understanding dad. "All you have to do is take that thing you used to play with when you were a little boy and stick it where your wife urinates."

"Wow, that sounds easy enough. Thanks, Dad," the boy said confidently. So he hung up the phone and threw his G.I. Joe doll in the toilet.

•

Define wet dream.
Coming unscrewed.

OLD AGE

What do old men do?
Luckfuck.

•

A very old man prepared to leave his exclusive London men's club. He drew on his overcoat, pulled his bowler down over his ears, wrapped his muffler warmly about his neck, and stepped out into the cold winter night. Tottering around the corner, the old man was startled to hear a sultry voice speak up in the vicinity of his left ear. "Would you like to come home with me, sir?"

Adjusting his monocle, the old man saw that he was being addressed by a very tall black woman clad in thigh-high vinyl boots, a sequined minidress, and a fake leopard skin coat.

"Eh?" he sputtered, taking stock of the situation. "All the way to Africa?"

•

Some time after his wife of thirty years had died, Leonard decided that he'd like to remarry. Soon afterward he met Sylvia and proposed to her.

Sylvia laid it on the line. "Leonard," she said, "there are some things I'm not prepared to live without if I marry you. First of all, I need a condominium in Florida."

"No problem. I've got a gorgeous condo in St. Pete," said the old man.

"Also, I need my own bathroom."

"Two and a half baths at my house—you get your choice."

Then Sylvia looked Leonard straight in the eye. "And sex?" she asked.

"Infrequently," answered the old man.

Thinking it over, Sylvia said, "Is that one word or two?"

•

The two old coots were both only a year short of retirement from the assembly line, but that didn't keep Joe from boasting to Manny, one Monday morning, about his sexual endurance.

"Three times," gasped Manny admiringly. "How'd you do it?"

"It was easy." Joe looked down modestly. "I made love to my wife, and then I rolled over and took a ten-minute nap. When I woke up, I made love to her again and took another ten-minute nap. And then I put it to her again, can you believe it! I woke up this morning feeling like a bull, I tell you."

"I gotta try it," said Manny. "Lorraine won't believe it's happening." So that night he made love to his wife, took a ten-minute nap, made love to her again, took another nap, woke up and made love to her a third time, then rolled over and fell sound asleep. Waking up feeling like a million bucks, he pulled on his clothes and ran to the factory, where he found his boss waiting outside for him. "What's up, Boss?" he asked. "I've been working for you for twenty years and never been late once. You aren't going to hold these twenty minutes against me now, are you?"

"What twenty minutes?" growled the boss. "Where were you Tuesday? Where were you Wednesday?"

•

When old Mr. O'Leary died, an elaborate wake was planned. In preparation, Mrs. O'Leary called the undertaker aside for a private little talk. "Please be sure to fasten his toupee to his head very securely. No one but I knew he was bald," she confided, "and he'd never rest in peace if anyone found out at this point. Our friends from the old country are sure to hold his hands and touch his head before they're through paying their last respects."

"Rest assured, Mrs. O'Leary," comforted the undertaker. "I'll fix it so that toupee will never come off."

Sure enough, the day of the wake the old timers were giving O'Leary's corpse quite a going-over, but the toupee stayed firmly in place. At the end of the day, a delighted Mrs. O'Leary offered the undertaker an extra thousand dollars for handling the matter so professionally.

"Oh, I couldn't possibly accept your money," protested the undertaker. "What's a few nails?"

•

Talking to his friends on the front porch, ninety-two-year-old Ed reports, "I've got my health. My heart is strong, my liver is good, and my mind, knock wood . . . Who's there?"

•

Seventy-three-year-old Sol had worked in the garment center all his life, and never found the time to get married. But one day a beautiful seventeen-year-old girl walked into the store and it was love at first sight. Within a month Sol and

85

Rachel were married and on the way to Florida for their honeymoon.

"So how was it?" asked Herschel, Sol's partner, when the couple returned.

"Oh, just beautiful," replied the starry-eyed Sol. "The sun, the surf . . . and we made love almost every night, we—"

"Just a minute," interrupted Herschel. "At your age, forgive me for asking, you made love almost every night?"

"Oh, yes," said Sol, "we almost made love Saturday, we almost made love Sunday. . . ."

•

Two old codgers were walking on the boardwalk and one said to the other, "I've gotta run home—time to make love to my wife."

His friend was astonished. "Eighty-eight you are, nearly as old as me, and you're rushing home to make love to your wife? What is this?"

"Our sex life is great, I gotta tell you," said the first guy, blushing a bit. "We make love two, maybe, three times a day."

"You're kidding me. How do you do it?" asked his friend.

"Pumpernickel bread, that's my secret," whispered the first man. And he tottered off toward home as fast as he could.

Hmmm, thought the first guy as he walked past a bakery, maybe I should try it. What do I have to lose? Going inside, he asked the woman at the counter if she had any pumpernickel bread.

"Yes, sir," she told him cheerfully. "We have shelves of it, in fact."

"So give me all of it." He decided.

"All of it, sir? It'll get hard."

"How come," sputtered the old man, "*everybody* knows about this but me?"

•

86

A retired couple was sitting at the table after their Sunday lunch when the wife looked over and said, "Know what I feel like? Ice cream. Will you go get me some?"

"Okay, honey," said the long-suffering husband, getting up.

"But not just any ice cream," she interrupted, "a sundae."

"Okay, dear, a sundae it is."

"But not just any sundae, a banana split. Should I write it down and put the note in your coat pocket?"

"No, dear," said the husband, pulling on his coat. "You want a special sundae, a banana split."

"Right, but not just any banana split. I want a scoop of chocolate on one side and a scoop of vanilla on the other. Sure you don't want me to write it down?"

"I got it, I got it," said the beleagered husband, heading for the door.

"But that's not all," she shouted after him. "I want it to be special. I want whipped cream and a cherry on top. Let me write it down for you."

"No, no, no," protested her husband. "You want a special ice cream sundae: a banana split with a scoop of vanilla here, a scoop of chocolate there, some whipped cream, and a cherry on top."

"And don't forget the chopped nuts."

"Chopped nuts," repeated the husband as the door closed after him.

Two hours later the husband returned and put a greasy paper bag on the kitchen table. The wife walked over, looked inside, and saw four bagels. Looking up at him in intense irritation, she snapped, "I knew it—you forgot the cream cheese."

RELIGIOUS

Father Callahan was concerned with the decreasing attendance at his Sunday Mass, and decided he should try to spice it up with a few more timely topics. So the next Sunday he startled his audience with the question, "Has anybody here ever seen a ghost?"

Almost a third of the congregation's hands went up.

"And how many of you have actually spoken to a ghost?" asked the priest from his pulpit.

At this point, only eight hands remained raised.

Father Callahan smiled mysteriously. "And how many of you have had sexual relations with a ghost?"

One hand stayed up, and the priest was none too pleased to see that he was now addressing Paddy O'Bryan, the town drunk. "Paddy," he asked gently, "have you actually had sex with a ghost?"

"Oh, no," admitted Paddy with an abashed smile. "I thought you said 'goat.'"

•

Why didn't Christ push the stone back in front of his tomb on Easter morning?

Well, he *was* born in a barn. . . .

•

Art and Bert happened to die and arrive at the pearly gates simultaneously. St. Peter greeted them warmly but confessed to a slightly embarrassing problem. "Heaven happens to be completely full right now," he admitted, "and I'm afraid you won't be able to be admitted for two weeks or so."

"What?" yelped Art and Bert. "We were good all our lives. Why should we be penalized at this point?"

"Listen, we'll make it up to you," offered St. Peter, leaning toward them conspiratorially. "You two can go back to earth in any form you choose, and we'll send someone for you the minute there's room."

Art and Bert agreed to the deal, and Art stepped right up and requested to be turned into an eagle in Colorado. *Poof!* He vanished. "Done," said St. Peter, dusting off his hands and turning to Bert. "How about you?"

"I'd like to be a stud in L.A." And—*poof!*—Bert disappeared.

A few weeks later St. Peter summoned an angel and instructed him to fetch the two men. "Fine," said the angel, "but how will I know them?"

"The first guy should be easy. There aren't very many eagles in Colorado to begin with, and the one flying the highest is sure to be him," advised St. Peter.

"And the second one?"

"That's going to be trickier," St. Peter admitted. "There have been a lot of building projects in Los Angeles lately."

•

Why's Jesus such a lousy lover?

It's been over a thousand years and he's only come once.

•

90

When Sister Margaret died, she was astonished to find herself in hell. Running to the phone, she called up St. Peter and reminded him of her excellent heavenly credentials. "There's been a terrible mistake," she warned him. "I'm a *nun,* and I'm counting on you to get me out of here immediately."

St. Peter assured her he would get right on it. But when two days had gone by with no change, Sister Margaret called him up again and delivered a tirade. "You've got to get me out of here!" she screamed.

"Okay, Sister, okay," reassured St. Peter. But another two days went by to no effect, and he got another call from Sister Margaret. "They're having a sex show down here tomorrow," she screeched, nearly hysterical, "and you positively have to get me out of here first."

"I'm working on it," said St. Peter, but he didn't give her another thought until the phone rang a few days later.

"Hey, Pete," said a husky voice, "Maggie here. You can forget about those earlier phone calls."

•

The Pope decided to visit America and was gratified to see a huge crowd waiting for him at JFK Airport. But it was disconcerting to hear them chanting, "Elvis! Elvis! Elvis!" as he stepped down from the plane. "Oh, my children, thank you," he said, bowing his head modestly. "But I am not Elvis."

No one seemed to hear him, and he was ushered into a white stretch limo with "Elvis" written in diamonds on the doors. "Bless you," he said to the sequined chauffeur, "but I am not Elvis."

When the limo pulled up to the Waldorf, it had to make its way through a huge crowd crammed behind police barricades, all chanting, "Elvis! Elvis! Elvis!"

Shaking his head, the Pope followed his luggage to the most sumptuous suite in the hotel. As he was unpacking, the door behind him opened and in walked three lovely women clad in the scantiest of negligees. The Pope looked them over for a moment or two, cleared his throat, and began to sing, "Well, it's one for the money, two for the show . . ."

•

Why do the Ayatollah Khomeini's children hate their mother?
Because she's a mullah-fucker.

•

Little Jimmy decided to make some money during spring vacation by selling Amsterdam cheese door-to-door. Pretty soon he came up to the minister's house, and when the rector answered the door, he asked, "Do you want to buy some 'dam cheese?"

"Hey there, little boy," chided the minister, "you know you shouldn't be talking like that."

"It's short for Amsterdam," explained Jimmy.

"Oh, I see. Well, in that case, I'll take half a pound." The minister put the cheese in the fridge, bringing it out for dinner that night with his family. "Son, pass the 'dam cheese, please," he asked politely.

"Now you're talkin', Dad," yelled his son. "Pass the fuckin' butter!"

•

Old Mrs. Watkins awoke one spring morning to find that the river had flooded not only her basement, but the whole first floor of her house. And, looking out her bedroom window, she saw that the water was still rising.

Two men in a passing rowboat shouted up an invitation to row to safety with them.

"No thank you," answered Mrs. Watkins tartly. "The Lord will provide." The men shrugged and rowed on.

By evening the water had risen so much that Mrs. Watkins was forced to climb out onto her roof, where she was spotted by a cheerful man in a motorboat. "Don't worry, lady," he yelled across the water, "I'll pick you right up."

"Please don't bother—the Lord will provide." And Mrs. Watkins turned her back on her would-be rescuer. "Suit yourself," he said, buzzing off.

Pretty soon Mrs. Watkins was forced to take refuge on her chimney, the only part of her house which was still above water. Fortunately a Red Cross cutter came by on patrol. "Jump in, lady. We'll save you," urged a rescue worker.

"No, thank you," said Mrs. Watkins. "The Lord will provide." So the boat went on, the water rose, and Mrs. Watkins drowned. Dripping wet and quite annoyed, she came through the pearly gates and demanded to see God. "What happened?" she demanded furiously. "I thought the Lord would *provide*."

"For cryin' out loud, lady," answered God wearily, "I sent *three boats*."

•

Two nuns happened to be avid football fans, but at a big game they had the misfortune of being seated in front of two really drunk, obnoxious guys. "I think I'll move to Utah," yelled one loudly. "I hear there aren't too many Catholics there."

"Good idea," hooted his companion. "How about California, though?" I hear there're hardly *any* Catholics there."

One of the nuns turned around to the two louts, who were convulsed by their own wit. "Why don't you both go to hell?" she snapped. "There are *no* Catholics there."

•

What's the most elastic substance in the world?

The human skin. In the Bible, it says Jesus tied his ass to a tree and walked 300 yards.

•

A Protestant minister deplaned at Kennedy airport from Belfast and hailed a cab to take him into Manhattan. As it turned out, the driver happened to be an Irish Catholic.

"Please take me to Christ Church in New York City," the minister requested.

"No problem," responded the cabbie as he headed across the Van Wyck Expressway. Twenty minutes later, the cab was heading up Fifth Avenue and finally came to a stop in front of St. Patrick's Cathedral.

"This isn't Christ Church!" complained the outraged Protestant.

"I've been driving these streets for over ten years," the Catholic driver told him. "If He's home at all, He'll be in there."

MISCELLANEOUS

Young Bobby needed eyeglasses but he refused to wear them. "But son," urged his dad, "you'll be able to see so much better."

"I can see just fine, Dad," protested Bobby. "Why, I can see that dog coming up the street three blocks away, and I can tell he has only one eye."

"Bobby," said his father in exasperation, "that dog isn't going up the street, it's going down the street."

•

Did you hear about the neat nurse?

She made the patient without disturbing the bed.

•

A tipsy guy in a bar stood up and made the following speech: "I am white from head to toe. I am rich, I am handsome, and my name is Brown. B-R-O-W-N."

Thoroughly annoyed, Sam retorted: "My name is Sam

and I am white from head to toe, except my rectum, which is brown. B-R-O-W-N."

•

Why shouldn't the number 288 ever be mentioned in polite company?

It's two gross.

•

Two fishermen were accustomed to fishing alongside one another every weekend, but they never exchanged any words. Then, one weekend, one of them failed to appear. Nor did he show the next weekend. But on the third Saturday, he was back in his usual spot.

"Missed you," said the first fisherman.

"Got married."

Half an hour later the first one said, "She must be something to keep you off fishing for two weekends. Is she that beautiful?"

"Nothing special," said the newlywed.

Half an hour later the first man spoke up again. "She a good cook?"

"If you like frozen food."

In due course came the next question. "She must be dynamite in bed then, eh?"

"Same as all the rest," said the second fisherman, shrugging offhandedly.

"So why'd you marry her?" demanded the first, unable to contain himself.

"She's got worms."

•

Miss Tucker decided that the second grade had been so well behaved that day that she'd let them draw on the blackboard. As soon as she announced her plans to the class,

Dirty Eddie's hand shot up, but she ignored him and let Lucy go first.

"I'm going to draw a cabin on a mountain," announced the little girl, and drew this.

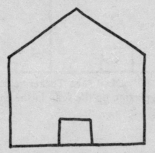

Lucy sat down and Miss Tucker looked for someone to call on besides Dirty Eddie, who was still waving his hand. "Alice, you may go."

"Since the cabin is on a mountain, it should have snow on it," pronounced Alice as she added this to the drawing.

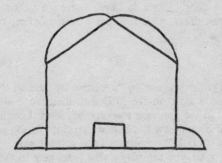

As Alice took her seat, the teacher had no choice but to choose Dirty Eddie. He proceeded to the blackboard and drew this.

"And what is that?" asked Miss Tucker reluctantly.

"That's my Dad picking up the soap in the shower," said Dirty Eddie.

•

John came home from work an hour earlier than usual and was somewhat surprised to find his wife stark naked in bed. "What's up, honey?" he asked.

"I'm protesting because I don't have anything to wear," was her explanation.

"Now honey, that's ridiculous," said John, pulling open the closet door. "Look in here. There's a yellow dress, a flower-print dress, your new pants suit, hi, Jim, your pink housedress . . ."

•

The avid golfer was out on the course with his wife one day. He played a shot on the fifth that sliced so badly that it ended up in the gardener's equipment shed. Looking in the door, the couple saw the ball sitting right in the middle of the room. "Look," volunteered the golfer's wife, "if I hold the door open, you can play a shot from here to the green."

This struck the golfer as an interesting challenge, but alas, the ball missed the open door and struck his wife on the temple, killing her instantly.

Many years later the widower was playing with a friend when he hit the exact same slice. The two of them walked into the shed, and sure enough, there sat the ball in the center of the room. "I tell you what," said the friend. "If I hold the door open, I bet you can get the ball back onto the green."

"Oh, no," said the golfer, shaking his head. "I tried that once before and it took me seven shots to get out."

•

What do outhouses and candy have in common?
If there's no hole, it's not a lifesaver.

•

What's a 10,085?
Sixty-nine with the U.S. Marine Corps watching.

•

The members of a ladies' club were offended by the vulgar language consistently used by one of its members, and decided among themselves to walk out of the room at the next occasion. At a meeting the very next week, the offending member walked in and loudly asked, "Hey, girls! Did you hear the Army is advertising for a shipload of women to go overseas to service the troops?"

In unison the whole roomful of women stood up. As they reached the door, they heard, "No need to rush—the ship isn't leaving till next week!"

•

A worker on the construction site of a highrise climbed all the way to the top of the building before he realized he needed a second set of hands for the job he had in mind. Not wanting to climb all the way back down, and realizing that no one would hear him if he yelled, he signaled to the foreman on the ground. He pointed first to himself, then to his knee, then to the foreman, meaning, "I need you."

The foreman waved back but then started acting very

strangely: he unzipped his pants, pulled them down to his ankles, and began to jerk off. Totally confused and rather alarmed, the worker ran down all fourteen stories of the highrise, staggered over to the foreman, and gasped, "What the hell did you mean?"

"I got your message," the foreman explained, "and I just wanted to let you know I was coming."

•

Little Freddy was mad at the world. He went for a walk, and when a chicken came up to him and pecked at his knee, Freddy kicked it as hard as he could. Then a cow came up to him and her wet breath bugged him, so he kicked her as hard as he could. And when a pig came up and grunted at him, Freddy sent it squealing with another vicious kick.

He hadn't realized that his mother had witnessed all of these scenes, and she asked for a word with him when he got home. "For kicking the chicken, no eggs for a week," Freddy's mother pronounced sternly. "For kicking the cow, no milk for a week, and for kicking the pig, no bacon for a week."

Late that afternoon the little boy's father came home in such a bad mood that he kicked the cat halfway across the room. Turning to his mother, Freddy asked, "Want me to break the bad news to Dad?"

•

There once was a fellow who liked to drop in at the local tavern on his way home from work and have a few with the guys. Frequently, though, he'd end up drunk, and would stagger home to be met at the door by his suspicious wife. She'd lean over as if to kiss him, but if she smelled booze on his breath, she'd slap him on the face.

One drunken evening, the man decided he'd taken enough slaps in the face and was going to outsmart his wife. Stopping at the corner market, he bought a can of sardines to eat on the way home. At his front door his wife leaned over as usual to give him a kiss, and the guy figured he had it made. But instead she hauled back and slapped him harder then ever, screaming, "*Damn* you—I break you of one bad habit and you go and take up another!"

•

A timid tourist stopped a New York City cop. "Can you tell me how to get to Carnegie Hall," she asked, clearing her throat nervously, "or should I just go fuck myself?"

•

A father was driving to town with his eleven-year-old son when the kid popped open the glove compartment and came across a box of rubbers. "What're these, Dad?" the kid asked innocently.

"Those are, uh, rubbers," stammered his father, "and . . . they're for putting on cigarettes to make them taste better."

No sooner had they arrived in town than the boy ran into the nearest drugstore and asked the clerk for some rubbers.

"What size?" asked the clerk.

The boy thought for a moment, then answered, "Big enough to fit a Camel."

•

It was time for the third grade's weekly vocabulary study. "Today, class, the study word is 'definitely', announced Mrs. Ripley, "and I want each of you to make up a sentence using that word correctly. Now you can ask me a question, but *only* if it applies to the use of the study word in your sentence. Okay? You may raise your hands when you're ready, and we'll start our sentences."

Of course nasty little Petey's hand was the first to shoot up, but the teacher called on the girl sitting in front of him. "The sky is cloudy and it is *definitely* going to rain," she said primly and sat down.

"Very good, Louise," said the teacher. By this time Petey's hand was waving frantically, and Mrs. Ripley gave in.

"Teacher, I have a question for you first," said Petey.

"Fine," she said, "but remember—it must apply to the use of the study word."

"No problem," said the little boy. "My question is . . . is a fart lumpy?"

"Now, Petey," said Mrs. Ripley indignantly, "I made it quite clear that the question had to do with the word 'definitely'."

"Oh, but it *does*," Petey assured her.

So the teacher reluctantly gave in once more. "No, Petey, a fart is not lumpy."

"Well then," said Petey, looking down, "if a fart is not lumpy, I have *definitely* shit in my pants."

•

There was once a man with an insane passion for baked beans. They had the predictable effect on his digestive system, but he felt this was a small price to pay—until he fell in love. When they decided to marry, the man realized that such a refined and delicate woman would never put up with his unattractive habit, so he made the supreme sacrifice and gave up beans. They were married shortly thereafter.

Some months later his car broke down on his way home from work, so he called his wife to say he'd be walking home, and on the way he passed a little restaurant from which emerged a tantalizing aroma of baked beans. Figuring that he'd have several miles in which to work off the ill effects, he indulged in a big bowl. He put-putted all the way home and on arriving felt reasonably safe that he had farted his last.

"Darling," exclaimed his wife at the door, "I have the most wonderful surprise for dinner tonight. She blindfolded him and sat him at the head of the dining-room table and, when the phone rang, made him promise that he wouldn't touch the blindfold while she was out of the room. Seizing the opportunity gratefully, he shifted to one leg and let one go. It turned out to be loud and as ripe as rotten eggs, and he fanned the air vigorously with his napkin, praying that the phone call would be a long one. Things had just returned to normal when he felt another one coming on, and it turned out to be a real prizewinner. Keeping his ear on the phone conversation, the man went on like this for ten minutes, until he knew from the click of the receiver that his period of freedom was over. He had just time to replace his napkin and fold his hands on it, in a picture of innocence for his wife's return. "I'm sorry I took so long, honey," she said. "You didn't peek, did you?"

He assured her that he had not, whereupon she removed the blindfold. And there was his surprise: twelve dinner guests sitting around the table all ready to sing "Happy Birthday!"

•

The mother of five-year-old Jimmy offered to keep an eye on his classmate, Laurie, while the girl's mother paid a call on a sick friend. Leaving both children in the playroom, she went to make their lunch, and on her return she was shocked to find both of them naked and her son standing on the little girl's head.

"Jimmy!" she cried. "What are you and Laurie doing?"

"Well, Mom, we took our clothes off and I got on top of her," Jimmy explained patiently. "Now, when does it start to feel good?"

•

Why did Pepperidge Farm start making exploding cookies?
    Because Pepperidge Farm dismembers!

•

Why is a convict before sentencing like a new bride?
    They both know it'll be hard, but they don't know for how long.

•

Lady: Does the tuba player really make that noise with his mouth?

Conductor: Well, I hope so.

•

Especially horny one night, Sam rolled over and nuzzled his wife. "How about it, honey?" he asked tenderly.

"Oh, Sam, I've got an appointment with the gynecologist tomorrow," said his wife, going on to explain that the doctor had requested that she abstain from intercourse for twenty-four hours before an appointment.

Sam sighed deeply and turned over to his side of the bed. A few minutes later he rolled back and asked hopefully, "You don't have a dentist appointment, do you?"

•

More great lies:

It's only a cold sore.

I'm from the government and I'm here to help you.

Some of my best friends are Jewish.

Black is beautiful.

I've had a vasectomy.

•

On the first day of kindergarten the teacher went around the room to learn everyone's name, and was astonished to hear a cute little boy give his name as "Jimmy Fuckbreak."

"I see," she said, after making him repeat it twice. Figuring him for a smart mouthed kid, she asked, "Tell me, Jimmy, do you have any brothers or sisters in this school?"

"Sure. My sister's in the fifth grade," was the answer.

So as soon as it was time for cookies and punch, the teacher slipped out and headed for the fifth-grade class-room. Opening the door, she asked loudly, "Do you have any Fuckbreaks in here?"

"Hell, no!" retorted a boy in the front row. "We don't even get recess."

●

What is a seventy-two?
Sixty-nine with three voyeurs.

●

A drunk got into a cab and asked the driver if there was room in front for a pizza and a six-pack.
"Sure," said the driver obligingly.
So the drunk opened the partition, leaned forward, and threw up.

●

Six-year-old Teddy came into the house with his hands cupped together and asked, "Mom, is there such a thing as boy grasshoppers?"
"Why, yes, honey. Why do you ask?"
"How about girl grasshoppers?" persisted Teddy.
Mrs. Englehardt had never discussed the birds and the bees with her son and was convinced of his complete innocence. And, not wanting to deal with the whole issue quite yet, she patted him on the head and answered, "No, dear."
"Just wondering," said Teddy, smiling sweetly. Turning away, he clapped his hands together and screamed, "FAGGOTS!"

●

One rainy day a little boy was riding his tricycle furiously around the house, pretending to be a bus driver. Squealing to a stop in the living room, he yelled, "All you fuckers off! Okay, all you fuckers on!" Next stop was the dining room. "Move to the back of the bus, you fuckers!" When he reached the kitchen, his mother couldn't believe her ears. "Move it, you fuckers! All you fuckers off!"

"*What* did you say?" she demanded. And when the little boy obligingly repeated himself, she belted him so hard he landed against the far wall.

Picking himself up, the little boy pronounced, "And it's fuckers like you who make the bus late!"

•

The same little boy asked his father one day why Mommy had bumps on her chest. Somewhat at a loss, his father replied, "Oh, those are Mommy's balloons, and when she dies they'll float her up to heaven."

A week later he was at the office when his secretary put through a frantic call from his son. "Daddy, Daddy," cried the little boy, "Mommy's dying!"

"Calm down, Ernie," soothed the father. "What makes you think Mommy's dying?"

"Because the mailman's blowing up her balloons," sobbed Ernie, "and she's screaming at God that she's coming."

•

A man walked into a whorehouse and said, "I want a girl."

"Harry, grease up Belinda," shouted the madam up the stairs. "That'll be one hundred dollars," she said, turning back to her customer.

"A hundred bucks!" protested the man. "That's a little steep for my budget."

"Harry, grease up Angelique," called up the madam without blinking an eye. "She's fifty dollars."

"Can't afford her either," confessed the man sadly.

"Harry, grease up Sophie!" The madam turned to her customer hopefully. "Twenty-five dollars?"

"Sorry," said the man, hanging his head.

"Well how much *do* you have?" asked the madam impatiently.

"Two bucks."

"Harry, grease up!"

•

When Mick raised his hand to ask the teacher if he could go to the bathroom, she snapped, "Back to your seat!" So he had no choice but to pull down his pants and shit in his hands.

When class was dismissed, the teacher came over to Mick and asked, "What's in your hands?"

"A leprechaun."

"Oh, really—may I see him?"

"Nope," said Mick defiantly. "You scared him away."

This struck the teacher as a matter for the principal, who came into the classroom, asked the same question, and got the same answer: "You can't see him either, 'cause you scared him away."

"That's it," snapped the principal. "I'm calling your parents."

Mick's mother couldn't get any more out of him. All eyes turned to Mick's big, husky father, who took his son firmly by the shoulders and asked, "What's in your hands, Mick?"

"A leprechaun," said the boy.

"Oh, yeah?" boomed his father. "Let me see him or you'll get a whipping that'll make your ears ring for a week!"

At that Mick opened his hands. "Jesus, Dad," he cried, "you scared the holy shit out of him!"

•

How many Americans does it take to screw in a light bulb?

One.

•

What do you call a kid raised in a whorehouse?

A brothel sprout.

•

Did you hear that A&P and Stop & Shop have merged? The new store's called Stop 'n' P.

•

During the Indian Wars a cavalry brigade led a charge against a tribe of Cheyenne warriors, completely decimating the Indians. At the end the only one left alive was the Indian chief. "Since you fought so bravely," said the cavalry officer, "I'm going to spare your life."

Just as the chief was trying to find words to express his gratitude, a mess of Indians came over the hill and completely wiped out the cavalry brigade. The only survivor was the officer, to whom the Indian said, "I'm not going to be as generous as you were—you're going to die. But you can have three wishes before I kill you."

The officer nodded, thought for a minute, and said, "I'd like to see my horse." The horse was brought around, the officer whispered in its ear, and the horse tore off, only to return in an hour or so with a luscious blonde on its back.

"Please feel free to make use of my teepee," offered the chief tactfully. When the officer emerged some time later, the chief asked about his second wish.

"I'd like to see my horse." Again the horse received a whispered command and galloped off, this time returning with a lovely redhead. Again the chief gestured graciously toward his teepee, and again waited an appropriate amount of time before inquiring as to his prisoner's last wish.

"I'd like to see my horse." This time when the horse was led up to him, the officer grasped its bridle firmly, pinched its lips with his other hand, and whispered fiercely, "Watch my lips—I said *posse*."

•

What's the difference between New Jersey and yogurt?"
  Yogurt has culture.

•

Is sex better than pot?
  It depends on the pusher.

•

How many bureaucrats does it take to screw in a light bulb?
  Two: one to screw it in and one to screw it up.

•

Did you hear about the butcher who backed into the meat grinder?
  He got a little behind in his work.

•

What do you get when you cross a banana with a comedian?
  Peels of laughter.

•

What increases in value when it's turned upside down?
  The number six.

•

If two's company and three's a crowd, what are four and five?
  Nine, stupid.

•

What's more amazing than a girl who can play piano by ear?
  A man who can fiddle with his whiskers.

•

What do you get when a rocket falls on your foot?
  Missiletoe.

•

When should you charge your batteries?
  When you don't have enough cash.

•

What do you call a boomerang that doesn't come back?
  A stick.

•

Why couldn't Mrs. Leprechaun have any children?
  Her husband had shamrocks.

•

Kid: Santa, how come you always say, "Ho, ho, ho?"
Santa: Because a prostitute charges, but a "ho" is free.

•

A father with three teenaged daughters found himself on duty one Friday night. When the doorbell rang he opened the door to find a young man who said, "My name's Joe, I'm here for Flo, we're going to the show, is she ready to go?" The father relayed the message upstairs and a few minutes later Flo came downstairs and went out with her date.

Not much later the doorbell rang again. "My name's Teddy," said the young man on the doorstep. "I've come to get Betty, we're going out for some spaghetti, is she ready?" The father passed this on, and down came Betty.

Just as he had settled himself in his chair, the doorbell rang again. The young man began, "My name's Chuck—"

"No way, dammit," shouted the father, and slammed the door.

•

How do we know computers have been around since biblical times?

Because Eve had an Apple and Adam had a Wang.

•

How do married couples do it doggie style?

Without all the licking and sniffing.

•

When Harry came home from work early and found his wife lying nude and the bed in complete disarray, he went berserk. Convinced she'd been fooling around, he went frantically through the house searching for his rival. There was nobody upstairs, but as he came running downstairs he noticed a man in a bathrobe passing by the kitchen window. Beside himself with rage, he ripped the refrigerator off the wall, threw it through the window, and crushed the man to death.

"You idiot!" screamed his wife. "That was our next-door neighbor."

Harry was so stricken with regret that he hanged himself and then found himself standing, with two other men, in front of St. Peter.

"How did you die?" St. Peter asked one of them.

"I was running to the store to get some milk for the kid before it closed," he explained, "when a refrigerator came out of nowhere and flattened me."

"What about you?" St. Peter turned to Harry.

"I'm afraid I'm the guy who killed him," said Harry remorsefully, and told of his suicide.

"And how did you die?" St. Peter asked the third man.

"Well, I was minding my own business in the refrigerator . . ."

•

What does a housewife from Malibu wear to a funeral?

Her black tennis dress.

•

Archie and Joe shared an apartment, and every day when Archie came home from work he asked, "What do you know, Joe?" And since their life was pretty uneventful, week after week went by during which Joe had nothing to say in answer to Archie's question.

Finally Joe decided to take matters into his own hands. He purchased a horse, and when it was delivered he asked the groom to put it in the bathroom. Then he asked the groom to kill it and put the horse's body in the bathtub. The groom obeyed his orders, but as he was going out the door he couldn't resist asking Joe about them.

"I live with this guy who's always asking me, 'Whaddaya know, Joe?'" explained Joe, "and I never know anything. Tonight I can tell him about the dead horse in the bathtub."

•

An elderly Kentucky farmer went in to see his lawyer and announced his intention to divorce his wife.

"Do you have any grounds?" asked the lawyer.

"Yep, a hundred and forty acres of bottom land."

The lawyer tried again. "Does she beat you up?"

"Nope. We both get up at the same time every morning."

"I see," said the lawyer. "She must be a nagger."

"Certainly not," retorted the farmer. "She's white."

•

Officer Kelly's patrol car had some engine trouble late one night, and when he reported it, the sergeant on duty told him to forget the last two hours of his shift and go home. His house was dark, so he tiptoed into the bedroom, stripped off his uniform, hung it up, and went over to the bed.

Just as he was about to get in, his wife piped up. "Honey, is that you? Listen, I have a throbbing headache and no medicine—would you go to the drugstore and get me some? Oh, and don't turn on the light, it'll hurt my eyes."

So Kelly felt his way back to the closet, fumbled for his uniform, and drove to the drugstore. And when he got up to the counter with some extra-strength aspirin, the druggist asked, "Say, Officer Kelly, want to let me know why you're dressed in a fireman's uniform?"

•

During their cross-country trip the tourist couple stopped for lunch at a small-town cafe in the Southwest. They sat down at the counter and while they were drinking their coffee a cowboy came in and headed for a vacant stool next to them. As he swung his leg over the stool, he farted loudly.

The tourist jumped to his feet. "Sir, how dare you fart before my wife!" he protested indignantly.

The cowboy got off the stool, removed his Stetson, and tipped it politely. "Shucks, ma'am," he said politely, "I'm awful sorry—I didn't know we were taking turns."

•

Heard any good insults lately? How about:

You're so ugly your mother ties pork chops around your neck so the dog'll play with you.

You're so fat you need shock absorbers on your toilet seat.

You're so fat if you could jump high you'd cause a solar eclipse.

You're so fat you have stretch marks on your bathtub.

•

Mr. Smith was so honored to be chosen for the Martian inquiry into the nature of life on Earth that he gave the little green investigator a warm handshake. In fact he was so overcome that he forgot to let go.

Almost an hour later the interview drew to a close with the following questions.

"Do you humans pee?"

"Yes, we certainly do," replied Smith.

"Do you shit?"

"Yes, we do," answered Smith, slightly embarrassed.

"Do you wipe yourself with something?"

"Why, of course. We use toilet paper."

"That's interesting," commented the Martian. "On Mars we use our hands."

•

Why can't pencils have babies?
   They have rubbers.

•

Read the new best-seller, called *You Can Be Replaced*?
   It's by A. Bigg Vibrator.

•

How did the mathematician cure his constipation?
   He worked it out with a pencil.

•

What's the biggest drawback of jungle life?
   Tarzan's foreskin.

•

In an attempt to explain the principles of economics to his young son, the tycoon posited, "Think of me as capital, your mother as management, the maid as labor, and your baby sister as the future." So the kid mulled it over till bedtime. That night he woke up and wandered around the house, finding his mother asleep, his father in bed with the maid, and the baby sucking her thumb.

The next morning he said brightly, "Dad, I've got it all figured out. While management sleeps, capital is screwing labor, and the future sucks!"

•

When God received the results of his special survey, He was very upset: they indicated that fifty percent of earth's population was regularly engaging in kinky sex. Unable to believe the report, He sent Gabriel down to conduct an investigation. But Gabriel came back with a long face. "It's even worse than we thought, Sir," the angel reported. "It's not fifty percent, it's a full ninety-eight percent of the people down there."

God put His face in His hands. "How'm I going to punish ninety-eight percent of the population?" He moaned.

"Hey, I've got an idea," offered Gabriel brightly. "Instead, how about rewarding the two percent who *aren't* having kinky sex?"

God thought this was a brilliant idea, and had the plaque made up. And you know what it said?

Oh, you didn't get one either. . .

•

What's the definition of constipation?
    A log jam.

•

How can you tell when a lawyer is lying?
    His lips are moving.

•

What's the difference between a parachute and a prophylactic?
    When a parachute fails, somebody dies.

TOO TASTELESS TO BE INCLUDED

What's the slimiest thing in the world?
Two eels screwing in a bucket of snot.

•

Two little black girls were walking down a back street in Mobile when they came across an old black woman sitting on her front porch eating a watermelon, her feet propped up on the railing.

"That woman ain't got no drawers on," pointed out one of the girls to her friend. "Does that keep it any cooler?" she shouted up to the porch.

"I don't know, chile," answered the old woman, "but it sho keeps the flies offa my watermelon."

•

The lecherous old fag could no longer restrain himself when he found himself alone with a friend's handsome son. First he started tonguing the boy's ear. "Do you know what I'm doing?" he whispered throatily.

"Mmmm," murmured the boy, so the fag progressed, moving his hand down into the boy's shorts. "Know what I'm doing now?" he wheezed.

"Mmm hmmm."

Thrilled, the queen turned the boy over and started giving it to him up the ass. "Know what I'm doing now?" he groaned in ecstasy.

"Yeah," answered the boy laconically. "You're catching AIDS."

•

What's the definition of gross?

When you open the refrigerator door and the rump roast farts at you.

•

What's yellow, has slanted eyes, and knocks on glass?

An Asian in a microwave.

•

When Suzie came home late one night with rice in her hair, her mother asked, "Where the hell have you been, at a wedding?"

"No, Ma," answered Suzie. "I was blowing this Japanese guy and he puked on me."

•

A woman with huge breasts was out for a walk when she was jumped by a man holding a gun. When he motioned for her to take off her blouse, she warned him he'd regret it, but he insisted. Next he made her take her bra off, and when a giant set of tits popped into view he began to get incredibly

118

excited. "Take your skirt off," he growled, ignoring her warnings that he leave off.

So off came the skirt, and then the panties, revealing an equally huge pussy, green and slimy and swarming with bugs. Shocked and repelled, he stepped back and let the gun fall to the ground.

Grabbing the gun, the woman pointed it at him, smiled broadly, and commanded, "Eat me."

•

What would Hitler have invented if he'd lived another six months?

The self-cleaning oven.

•

"Mommy, Mommy, I don't want lasagne for dinner."

"Shut up or I'll take off another layer of skin."

•

Two Cubans were applying for U.S. citizenship and the day came for their test at the Department of Immigration. "Who was the first President of the United States?" is the first question.

Looking down into his underwear where all the answers are written, the first Cuban answers confidently, "George Washington."

"And what are the colors of the American flag?" the official asks.

Looking down again, he answers, "Red, white, and blue."

After a few more questions, the immigration officer passes the first Cuban, congratulates him on his new citizenship, and turns to his companion.

"Listen, Fidel," whispers the second guy, "can I borrow your underwear?" Quickly changing in the men's room, he stands before the officer and is asked to name the First President of the United States.

"Uh . . . Fruit of the Loom," is his answer.

"I see," says the official sternly. "And the colors of the American flag?"

Stealing another look downward, the second Cuban answers, "Green and brown."

•

What's grosser than gross?

Two Siamese twins connected at the mouth when one throws up.

•

What do Ku Klux Klan members thank the good Lord for every night?

Sickle-cell anemia.

•

To conquer his shyness, Joe applied for entrance to the local nudist's colony. The receptionist instructed him to go upstairs, shower, and come back down carrying all his clothes. Turning scarlet with embarrassment, Joe asked if he couldn't keep *some* clothes on.

"Absolutely not," was the woman's frosty reply, so Joe headed up the stairs. Looking out the second-story window, Joe spied two women on the lawn wearing black panties. Rushing back to the front desk, he demanded to know why he had to strip completely naked when women were allowed to wear panties.

"That's impossible," maintained the receptionist, so Joe led her over to the window to see for herself.

The woman turned to him, all smiles. "Those aren't panties," she explained brightly, "they're flies."

Would you like to see your favorite tasteless jokes in print? If so, send them to:

Blanche Knott
% St. Martin's Press
175 Fifth Avenue
New York, N.Y. 10010

Remember, we're sorry, but no compensation or credit can be given. But we *love* hearing from our tasteless readers.